ALL YOU NEED TO KNOW....

THE BRITISH EMPIRE

BY PIERS BRENDON

CONTENTS

To Rupert and Christine
with love

INTRODUCTION

The sun never set upon the British Empire, its critics liked to say, because God didn't trust the British in the dark. The joke was a backhanded tribute to the astonishing achievement of the inhabitants of a small island kingdom off the European mainland. Beginning in the seventeenth century with a few colonial settlements and trading posts clinging like limpets to alien shores, and expanding dramatically thereafter by occupation and conquest, they created the greatest empire that the world had ever seen. In its Victorian heyday, when Britannia ruled the waves, it consisted of 58 countries with a population of 400 million. Covering fourteen million square miles, or about a quarter of the earth's surface, it was seven times larger than the territories of Rome at their greatest extent.

It grew even bigger at the end of the Second World War, immediately before its sudden demise. According to a remark attributed to Napoleon, "great empires die of indigestion". Britain's seaborne empire was indeed grossly over-stretched. It was a far-flung but loosely-amalgamated assortment of dominions and dependencies, connected only late in the day by telegraph lines, submarine cables and "All-Red Routes" for steamships and aircraft. The bloated Empire dwarfed its tiny base. As early as 1810, one writer described it as an "oak planted in a flower-pot".

A similar comment might be made about this book, which is an attempt to provide a concise political history of the British Empire for the guidance of the general reader. Needless to say, the subject has been dealt with exhaustively in heavy tomes and multi-volume accounts; but it is so vast and complex that even they cannot entirely encompass it. Moreover such extended treatments, weighed down by thick branches of knowledge festooned with interpretative ivy, can obscure understanding. Sometimes more does mean worse and too much information can cause confusion. In the case of the British Empire, it is often impossible to see the wood for the trees or, rather, the tree for the foliage.

Between these covers, by contrast, is a bonsai oak. It is trimmed and shaped to afford, in miniature form, a distinct picture of Britain's imperial story. The aim is to offer a clear chronological narrative peppered with character, anecdote and quotation, to bring the Empire to life and to explain its demise, and finally to assess its pros and cons in its own terms as well as with the benefit of hindsight. The time-frame, too, is truncated. It stretches from the late eighteenth to the mid-twentieth century, covering what might be called the adolescence, maturity and dissolution of the British Empire. Its origins are outlined in the first chapter and the book concludes with a sketch of its aftermath and of Britain's attempts, which still continue, to find a post-imperial role.

Opposite: a portrait of Sir Richard Grenville in 1571. Artist unkown

AN · DÑI · 1571·
ÆTATiS · SVÆ
· 29 ·

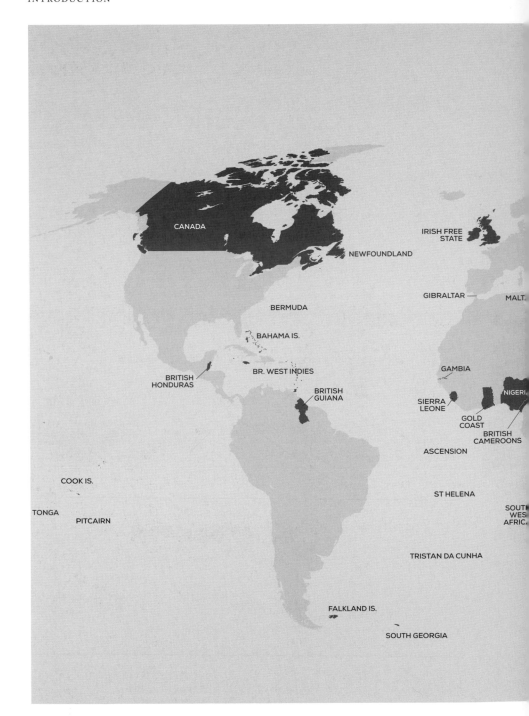

CANADA

NEWFOUNDLAND

IRISH FREE
STATE

GIBRALTAR —

MALT.

BERMUDA

BAHAMA IS.

BR. WEST INDIES

GAMBIA

BRITISH
HONDURAS

BRITISH
GUIANA

SIERRA
LEONE

NIGERI.

GOLD
COAST

BRITISH
CAMEROONS

ASCENSION

COOK IS.

ST HELENA

TONGA

SOUT
WES
AFRIC.

PITCAIRN

TRISTAN DA CUNHA

FALKLAND IS.

SOUTH GEORGIA

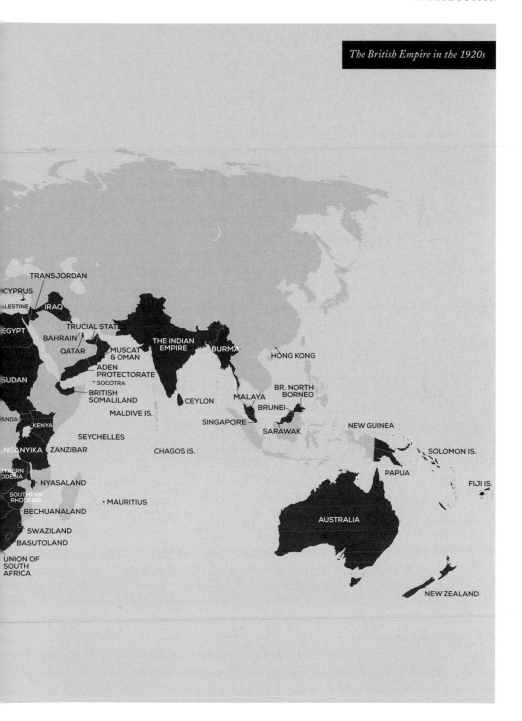

The British Empire in the 1920s

TRANSJORDAN
CYPRUS
LESTINE
IRAQ
EGYPT
TRUCIAL STATES
BAHRAIN
QATAR
MUSCAT
& OMAN
THE INDIAN
EMPIRE
BURMA
HONG KONG
ADEN
PROTECTORATE
SOCOTRA
SUDAN
BRITISH
SOMALILAND
BR. NORTH
BORNEO
CEYLON
MALAYA
BRUNEI
MALDIVE IS.
SINGAPORE
SARAWAK
ANDA
KENYA
NEW GUINEA
SEYCHELLES
NGANYIKA
ZANZIBAR
CHAGOS IS.
SOLOMON IS.
THERN
DESIA
PAPUA
FIJI IS.
NYASALAND
SOUTHERN
RHODESIA
MAURITIUS
BECHUANALAND
AUSTRALIA
SWAZILAND
BASUTOLAND
UNION OF
SOUTH
AFRICA
NEW ZEALAND

Chapter One

GENESIS OF EMPIRE

The British Empire, like other empires, was born of a desire to amass power and wealth. Following the loss of the crown's French dynastic possessions, England's subjugation and so-called "plantation" of Ireland was an early fulfilment of this craving. So was the exploratory voyage of John Cabot in 1497, a challenge to the Iberian monopoly of the New World. But none personified it more avidly than England's Elizabethan sea-dogs, who equated plunder with patriotism and profit with Protestantism – God helped those who helped themselves. John Hawkins, in 1562, became the father of the English slave trade, talking like a Puritan and taking as his crest a Moor bound with a cord. Martin Frobisher, Francis Drake and Richard Grenville were little more than pirates, the last of these being particularly rapacious and savage – he was said to crush wine glasses with his teeth and swallow them, "so that often times the blood ran out of his mouth without any harm to him".

Sir Walter Raleigh dreamed of El Dorado and the colony he established in Virginia in 1585 was mainly intended as a base for privateering. But he did promote the essential imperialist creed, namely that overseas colonies would prove a source of strength to the mother country, furnishing raw materials (notably naval supplies), affording a market for her own goods, and providing a depository for surplus population, especially paupers and convicts.

Commerce thus fostered, defended by the wooden walls of British ships and later protected by laws (the Navigation Acts) excluding foreign competitors, would become the lifeblood of the nation. As one prominent merchant said, trade was "a kind of war".

During the seventeenth century Britain's chief enemy was Holland, which took over from Spain and Portugal as the great maritime power and monopolised the immensely valuable spice trade. On the last day of 1600 Queen Elizabeth signed the charter of the East India Company, whose main business was to challenge Dutch supremacy. One of the directors wrote that it might seem silly to fight the Hollanders over pepper but it would be "a war for the Dominion of the British as well as the Indian seas". For if the Dutch became sole masters of pepper (vital for making European salted meat palatable), as they were of nutmeg, mace, cloves and cinnamon, they could pay for an invincible navy.

The struggle for dominance in the Far East was ferocious and the Dutch thought nothing of brutalising and executing English prisoners. Indeed, prior to the 1623 Amboyna Massacre they practised a version of "waterboarding", asserting that this was acceptable as "ordinary torture" in contrast to illegitimate "extraordinary and cruel torture" – a similar distinction was made by the British in Kenya during the 1950s and more recently by Americans who claim that waterboarding is simply an "enhanced interrogation technique".

Barred from the Spice Islands, the East India Company established trading stations at Madras, Bombay and Calcutta, on the fringe of the Mughal Empire. This was a byword for power, culture and magnificence, with a population of 100 million, about seventeen times larger than that of the British Isles, an elephant cavalry that would have astonished Hannibal and textile manufactures which clothed huge regions of Asia and Africa. When the London merchants presented the Emperor Jahangir (meaning World-seizer) with a splendid coach he had its iron fittings replaced with fittings of silver and gold; and they found to their chagrin that India wanted no goods from them, only bullion. It seemed inconceivable that a handful of white traders thousands of miles from their island home could translate their precarious commercial hold on India into military dominion, let alone found an oriental empire greater than that of Alexander or Augustus.

Nor did the settlements lodged haphazardly on the other side of the globe, in the West Indies and on the seaboard of North America, promise anything much in the way of empire. With the exception of the religious exodus, epitomised by the Pilgrim Fathers who sailed to New England in 1620 to gain freedom of conscience, Britons crossed the Atlantic for economic reasons. Colonies (such as Barbados and Baltimore) were private enterprises established with royal sanction, though Oliver Cromwell began to promote them as a matter of state policy. They were designed to augment the mother country's treasure by foreign trade. Especially valuable was the "triangular trade": English manufactures such as guns, knives, cloth and rum were exchanged for slaves in West Africa, who were transported to the New World in such ghastly conditions that a fifth of them died during this "Middle Passage", the vessels then carrying home cargoes of sugar, rice, cotton and tobacco. Merchants, artisans, farmers, indentured labourers, trappers, explorers, prospectors, freebooters and others came to America for the sake of what they could get. Felons left their country, it was said, for their country's good.

By the eighteenth century France had become Britain's chief foe and colonial rival. It was, according to one London journal, "the universal cormorant, that would, if possible, swallow up the whole globe". As the Mughal Empire disintegrated in India the European adversaries fought to pick up the pieces, forging alliances with local rulers and relying on native mercenaries.

Luckily for the British, they had a leader of genius in the person of Robert Clive, an East India Company clerk who became a conquistador. Heroic, charismatic and so dynamic that he had to calm his nerves with opium, Clive was a master of what he called "tricks, chicanery, intrigues, politics, and the Lord knows what". By deception as much as force, he won the battle of Plassey in 1757 and crushed French opposition in the subcontinent. This led, since no responsible British rule was established, to an orgy of exploitation. So-called "nabobs" (a corruption of the Indian word "nawab", prince) gorged on "Plassey plunder". The rich province of Bengal was bled white and a third of the population died of hunger.

William Pitt the Elder, Prime Minister during the global struggle between England and France known as the Seven Years War (1756-63), described Clive as a "heaven-born general". But his military audacity was matched by that of James Wolfe, of whom King George II allegedly said, when the Duke of Newcastle objected to promoting a madman: "Mad, is he? Then I hope he will bite some of my other generals." Leading an amphibious force across the St Lawrence and scaling the Heights of Abraham, Wolfe defeated the French army in front of Quebec. He died on the battlefield and, his earlier scorched earth tactics forgotten, he was glorified as an imperial martyr. Wolfe's victory enabled his countrymen to wrest Canada from French control. But despite its abundance of timber, fish and fur, Britain actually considered handing back this frozen wilderness to France during the peace negotiations, in exchange

"The Death of General Wolfe". Benjamin West painted this romantic and propagandist painting in 1770.

for the rich sugar island of Guadeloupe.

Pitt helped to build an empire but he was not an empire builder. Eloquent and arrogant, with an "eye that would cut a diamond", he aimed to secure commerce through war. "When trade is at stake," he declared, "you must defend it or perish." Like many of his contemporaries, he was reluctant to shoulder the burden of guarding and administering overseas dependencies. It was to alleviate this burden during the 1760s that the mother country attempted to levy taxes on the 2.5 million people of the thirteen American colonies now established between the Atlantic and the Appalachians. The rough treatment proved disastrous. As Benjamin Franklin warned, the British Empire (a term he popularised) was as delicate as a "China Vase".

Neither the tax on stamps nor duties on items such as sugar and tea caused the Americans unbearable financial hardship. But they regarded the impositions of the Westminster parliament, to which they sent no members, as a violation of their natural rights as elucidated by the philosopher John Locke. "No Taxation without Representation" was more of a political than an economic

The meeting of Mir Jafar and Robert Clive after the Battle of Plassey, painted by Francis Hayman in 1757. Clive bribed Jafar, the commander in chief of the Nawab's army, to help him secure victory.

slogan. It was a cry of defiance against the oppression of King George III's ministers. Rather than submit to the cruel and arbitrary exercise of English legislative power, Thomas Jefferson said that he would lend his hand "to sink the whole Island in the sea". He adopted as his motto the remark attributed to a regicide Englishman: "Rebellion to tyrants is obedience to God." Patrick Henry dramatised the revolutionary spirit while mobilising American forces on the eve of the War of Independence: "Give me liberty or give me death."

After the "shot heard round the world" which opened hostilities at Lexington in 1775, British redcoats made such a "vigorous retreat", taunted Benjamin Franklin, that the "feeble Americans could hardly keep up with them". In fact a long and terrible struggle ensued. Other Europeans states, notably France, entered the fray and tilted the balance against Britain. In 1781, when the Royal Navy temporarily lost command of the sea to a French fleet, George Washington's motley and ill-disciplined army compelled General Cornwallis to surrender at Yorktown. On hearing the news the Prime Minister Lord North paced his Downing Street room in a state of acute agitation, exclaiming repeatedly: "Oh God! It is all over!"

It *was* all over in key respects. The Americans had revolted because they were such good Englishmen, wedded to the ideal of English liberty. It was according to this ideal, proclaimed the weightiest political thinker of the day, Edmund Burke, that the "British Empire must be governed". Colonial rule, he insisted, "foaming like Niagara" in the House of Commons, was a trust to be exercised for the benefit of subject people. They, with maturity, would attain the birthright of all adults – independence. Thus from the start advocates justified the Empire on the paradoxical ground that it was a self-liquidating concern, a body carrying within itself the ideological germ of its own destruction. Perhaps it is not surprising that Edward Gibbon, the historian of *The Decline and Fall of the Roman Empire*, described Burke as "the most eloquent and rational madman that I ever knew".

Another influential theorist cut at the roots of the Empire while it was under attack from the Americans. In *The Wealth of Nations* (1776) Adam Smith asserted that colonies sapped the strength of the mother country. They were a huge monopoly set up for the profit of the mercantile classes, a protectionist union of customers suited to "a nation whose government is influenced by shopkeepers". Britain's prosperity would be better achieved by free trade, he argued, and the huge post-war boom in transatlantic traffic seemed to prove him right. So did the 19th-century acquisition of a vast "invisible" or "informal" empire, a sphere of commercial penetration and political influence stretching from China to Argentina. Yet after the loss of the

American colonies Britain turned decisively towards territorial expansion and dominion. Rebuffed in the west, it secured possessions in the east which dwarfed the conquests of Napoleon.

How did this happen? The answers are deep-seated. Since 1688 Britain had enjoyed political and social stability as well as freedom of thought. It had been transformed by revolutions in agriculture, finance, commerce, technology and industry, outstripping the advanced empires of Asia. Thanks to longstanding agrarian improvements, Britain needed only one farm labourer to feed three factory hands. It developed sophisticated financial institutions and credit machinery. It pioneered naval innovation, Deptford dockyard becoming the largest industrial enterprise on the planet. By 1820 a Lancashire spinning-machine operative could produce up to fourteen times as much cotton yarn per hour as his Indian competitor. Whereas China suffered from food and fuel shortages, Britain possessed coal aplenty to fire its new steam engines. Thus chance, or Destiny, played its part in the genesis of the Empire. The Rev William Buckland, Professor of Mineralogy at Oxford, reckoned that Providence had placed coal and iron deposits together near Birmingham in order to make England the richest country on earth.

Sir Walter Raleigh by Nicholas Hilliard. Miniature portrait painted around 1584, the year Raleigh was knighted.

'Surrender of Cornwallis at Yorktown' by John Trumbull. Oil on canvas, 1820

ROBERT CLIVE 1725-1774

Robert Clive's precocious military talents were comparable to those of Napoleon and his conquests were more enduring. Born into a large, hard-up Shropshire landed family, Robert was addicted to fighting as a boy and in manhood he remained almost pathologically aggressive. Packed off to Madras at the age of seventeen, he became acutely depressed by his life as a "writer", or clerk, in the service of the East India Company and twice attempted to shoot himself. On both occasions his pistol misfired and he took this as a sign that he was destined for greatness. His opportunity came in 1746 when hostilities broke out against the French, then the paramount European power in the subcontinent. Clive exchanged the pen for the sword and immediately proved that he had been, as his commanding officer said, "born a soldier".

Combining molten passions and a will of iron, he inspired his troops, who were mainly sepoys, though he spoke no Indian tongue. He led them through several victorious campaigns culminating in the capture and defence of Arcot in 1751, when he routed a vastly superior force including armoured elephant cavalry. Clive was chiefly responsible for destroying French ascendancy in south India and he was hailed as a hero at home. Here he used the fortune that he had acquired, mainly through supplying the army, to enrich his family, purchase property and procure political influence. But he provoked enmity by his greed, petulance and ambition.

In 1757 the Nawab of Bengal, Siraj ud-Daulah, seized the Company's Calcutta trading post and confined British prisoners in the notorious Black Hole, where a number of them died. Clive relieved the city and forcibly prevented the French from allying with the Nawab, whom he defeated at the battle of Plassey. Employing Indian puppets, Clive now became master of Bengal, which was ruthlessly exploited by servants of the Company. Clive himself, as T. B. Macaulay wrote, "walked between heaps of gold and silver, crowned with rubies and diamonds, and was at liberty to help himself". He took well over £100 million in modern money and said that he was astonished at his own moderation.

More important were the tax-collecting and administrative powers that the Company gained. Thinking ahead, Clive aimed to end rapacity and impose sovereignty. It was "scarcely a hyperbole to say that the whole Mogul Empire is in our hands," he wrote in 1765, proposing that the British should become the undisguised rulers of India. Clive never saw the raj whose foundations he had laid, dying by his own hand at the age of forty-nine.

Above: Portrait of Robert Clive by Nathaniel Dance. Date unknown.

Chapter Two

BIRTH OF THE RAJ

In America Britain lost colonies of occupation but in India it gained an imperial raj. The British raj (meaning rule) was primarily achieved by force of arms; and it was established between Clive's victory at Plassey in 1757 and the suppression of the so-called Indian Mutiny exactly a hundred years later, which resulted in the institution of crown control. During this century the East India Company managed the administration and conducted the expansion of British power. It seized tax revenues and formed private armies of sepoys.

These Indian troops, equipped with firelocks and bayonets, uniformed in blue turbans, red jackets and white drawers, abandoned tom-toms and trumpets and marched to the beat of the fife and the drum. They obeyed orders given in English and would make India, as one historian wrote, "an English barrack in the Oriental seas". They provided a cost-free standing army which served abroad (between 1789 and 1946) as well as in India itself. The Company thus eventually subjugated about two-thirds of the subcontinent (leaving the rest to some 600 subservient rajahs and maharajahs) in what the author William Dalrymple describes as "the supreme act of corporate violence in world history".

The Westminster parliament made periodic attempts to regulate the East

India Company, notably in 1773 when it faced bankruptcy. That was thanks to the American boycott of its tea and the unbridled rapacity of its own servants in India who, it was said, "to get a rupee would sell an army". The Hindi word "loot" soon became common currency in England where fortunes made in India, as T. B. Macaulay said, inflated the price of everything from fresh eggs to rotten boroughs. In the words of a capable Company official, Warren Hastings: "The dominion exercised by the British Empire is fraught with many radical and incurable defects." In 1774 he was charged to remedy them and appointed the first Governor-General of India. Hastings was mocked as the clerk who sat on the Mughals' throne.

He did act somewhat in the manner of the Emperor Jahangir, with brilliantly calculated ruthlessness. He pillaged rich provinces. He played off one local ruler against another and hired out his sepoy army to maharajahs who could pay for it. He faced down English opponents and dealt harshly with Indian foes, having one of them judicially murdered. Moreover he ignored the injunction, formulated in William Pitt the Younger's India Act (1784), not to extend the Company's rule in the subcontinent, knowing that the British must win power or lose commerce. On his return home Hastings was impeached for peculation and misgovernment, Edmund Burke charging that he was "the captain-general of iniquity" who had never dined without creating a famine. After a seven-year trial Hastings was acquitted. For all his faults, he had imposed a degree of order on India, whose culture he respected and whose people respected him. As the historian Percival Spear concluded: "He found a revenue administration and left a state."

Between 1786 and 1793 his austere, upright and narrow-minded successor Lord Cornwallis transformed India into a *British* state. At this time many Britons in India were (in the opprobrious Victorian term, which nevertheless indicates that imperialism was a profoundly reciprocal process) "going native". They smoked hookahs, wore dhotis, sprouted moustaches, chewed betel, ate curry, drank arrack, attended nautches (dances), kept local mistresses and deemed cows sacred. But Cornwallis believed that Indians were incorrigibly decadent and corrupt, and he dismissed them from high official positions. In their place he appointed Englishmen, forbidding those in political service to trade and laying down the high standards of probity which so distinguished the Indian Civil Service during the 19th and 20th centuries.

Exploitation persisted, the *raison d'être* of the raj. But in the wake of the Hastings trial, the notion of imperial trusteeship was born, of civilised Europeans governing "lesser breeds" (Rudyard Kipling's phrase) for their own good. Retrieving in Calcutta a reputation lost at Yorktown, Cornwallis

Government House in Calcutta, 1860s. It was the residence of British Governors-General and Viceroys until 1911.

instituted all sorts of paternalistic reforms. Most notably he established a new legal code which was more enlightened than that which prevailed at home. He was hailed as the "Justinian of India".

Lord Wellesley, elder brother of the future Duke of Wellington, was appointed Governor-General in 1797 and came to dominate more of India than even the greatest Mughal emperor. He was accordingly described as "the Akbar of the Company's dynasty".* Intent on eradicating all traces of French revolutionary influence and thwarting Napoleon's eastern designs, Wellesley pursued an aggressive "forward policy". "I will heap kingdoms upon kingdoms, victory upon victory, revenue upon revenue," he boasted, "I will accumulate glory and wealth and power." He added much to the raj, brought princely states under the Company's "protection" and defeated Tipu Sultan, the "Tiger of Mysore". Confiscating half his territory, Wellesley struck a medal showing the British lion overcoming the Indian tiger. He also decorated his throne with some of Tipu's jewels. Aspiring to imperial splendour, he built a huge, domed Government House in Calcutta. India was now to be ruled, as one contemporary said, "from a palace not from a counting house; with the ideas of a Prince, not those of a retail dealer in muslins and indigo".

Akbar was the greatest of the Mogul emperors

To assert his regal status and his fierce pride of caste, Wellesley held aloof from British as well as Indian society. Although so lecherous that his brother thought he ought to be castrated, he even shunned the company of women – perhaps because, in the heat, they were said to resemble painted corpses. "I stalk about like a Royal Tiger," he wrote, in "magnificent solitude". Apparently invisible was the ubiquitous host of servants and flunkeys. The Company recalled Wellesley in 1805, deploring his extravagance and belligerence. But although his expansionist policy was temporarily reversed, it had a juggernaut momentum of its own. The battles of Trafalgar and Waterloo established British global supremacy for a century. And over the next two decades, in search of security and in the absence of any national resistance, the raj spread across south India. Forty thousand Britons controlled a fifth of the world's population.

Mercantile motives still predominated and as Britain became the workshop of the world demands for raw materials and foreign markets grew ever more insistent. But with military triumph and technological progress came an assumption of cultural and racial superiority, and a belief in Britain's civilising mission. Thus in 1807 parliament abolished the slave trade, a move which (Napoleon having reintroduced slavery) established Albion's claim to moral leadership of the world – after two and a half centuries during which English ships had transported 3.4 million slaves to the Americas.

India became a field for missionary endeavour. The first bishop of Calcutta was appointed in 1813, his diocese stretching from St Helena to Sydney. The conversion of the heathen was even more important, William Wilberforce reckoned, than stopping the traffic in human blood. Evangelical Christians were particularly appalled by "the idolatrous filth and obscenity" of Hinduism, which included "bull, peacock, monkey, and other nameless objects of worship".

There was also a drive to modernise India along utilitarian lines. A leading reformer was Lord William Bentinck, Governor-General between 1828 and 1835. He banned practices such as suttee (Hindu widow-burning) and thuggee (the ritual murder of travellers). He promoted steamboats, railways, trunk roads, postage, European medicine, an enlightened penal code and above all English education, including the teaching of English, "my panacea for the regeneration of India". In this Bentinck was supported by a brilliant member of his Council, the historian Thomas Babington Macaulay. Nicknamed "Babbletongue" since he talked incessantly – Lord Melbourne would have preferred to share the cabinet room, said the Duke of Wellington, with a chime of bells and ten parrots – Macaulay eloquently advocated

Britannia and her pets, the British lion and the Indian tiger, ready to take on Afghanistan. Punch cartoon (April 4, 1885)

READY!

a Western curriculum. If this revealed his contempt for Eastern culture it also expressed his hope that Indians (including Untouchables) would thus be trained for eventual independence. The ending of the raj would be the proudest day in our history, Macaulay declared, provided that Britons left behind an empire immune to decay, "the imperishable empire of our arts and our morals, our literature and our laws".

The policies of annexation and westernisation were so provocative that they might have brought the raj to a premature end in 1857. An aggressive effort to safeguard India's North West Frontier had already led to the first of several disastrous wars in Afghanistan, culminating in General Elphinstone's doomed retreat from Kabul in 1842. But while the British continued to stand against real and imagined Russian advances in the Himalayas, a prolonged confrontation known as the Great Game, they advanced on the plains.

This was especially so after 1848 when Lord Dalhousie became Governor-General, the haughtiest and most bellicose since Wellesley. He completed the conquest of the Punjab and seized the most spectacular piece of imperial loot, the Koh-i-noor Diamond, presenting it to Queen Victoria – its previous owner, the Maharajah Duleep Singh, duly christened her Mrs Fagin. Dalhousie found excuses to take over princely states and even occupied lower Burma as a bulwark to India. But he failed to reform the ill-treated sepoy army or to prevent the introduction of cartridges greased with pig and cow fat, offensive to both Hindus and Muslims. A hundred years after Plassey many regiments mutinied and vast swathes of northern India were ravaged by the "Devil's Wind".

The mutineers occupied Delhi. Altogether they killed over two thousand Britons, including women and children, the most notorious massacre taking place at Cawnpore. But they were never able to meld popular grievances into a national struggle, to turn a military uprising into a war of independence. With the help of railways, steamboats and the telegraph, the British mustered reinforcements, among them Sikhs and Gurkhas, and crushed the rebellion. Horrified that a subject race should violate the trust of its white masters, they succumbed to a pathological spirit of vengeance. Typical was Captain Garnet Wolseley who vowed to shed "barrels of the filth which flows in these niggers' veins for every drop of blood" they had spilled. In countless tens of thousands, sepoys and civilians accused of complicity were imprisoned, flogged, tortured, defiled, bayoneted, shot, hanged or blown from the mouths of guns. The retribution, which left an ineradicable legacy of bitterness, was far worse than the insurrection.

This was part of a familiar pattern. The British Empire was a weak empire:

The British Lion's vengeance on the Bengal Tiger after the Indian Mutiny.
Punch cartoon (22 August, 1857)

heterogeneous and incoherent, run on a shoestring, professing noble ideals and constitutionally averse to violence. To be sure it was mainly won by the sword. The Empire was not acquired "in a fit of absence of mind", as the historian J. R. Seeley said, but by a curious combination of accident and design, subjugation and occupation. Often it was not so much pushed out by competing authorities in Westminster and Whitehall as pulled out by the man on the spot, a pugnacious proconsul or an ambitious general. But the British preferred to rule by collaboration rather than coercion and only when their rule was challenged did they respond with ferocity.

After the Mutiny, Dalhousie's successor Lord Canning earned his nickname, "Clemency". As the first Viceroy of a crown government that superseded the Company raj, he sought reconciliation and consolidation. He issued an amnesty, ceased annexations, discouraged Christian evangelism, respected Hindu customs, and placated conservative landlords and maharajahs. In short, Canning abandoned the westernising policies of his predecessors. India would be administered firmly but the British yoke would be easy.

Chapter Three

DOMINION OF CANADA

The American and French revolutionary wars led to a dramatic expansion of the British Empire. After 1784 Canada was secured by the advent of United Empire Loyalists from the thirteen colonies and by conciliatory gestures from the imperial authorities in London. Since Britain could no longer send convicts to the New World, it exploited the discoveries of its greatest navigator James Cook and transported them to Australia – the first fleet arrived at Botany Bay in 1788 to inaugurate what one contemporary called a "Colony of Disgracefuls". When Irish rebels tried to take advantage of England's conflict with France, Pitt's government responded with repression and assimilation, ruthlessly incorporating "John Bull's other island" into the United Kingdom by the Act of Union (1800).

During the struggle against Napoleon Britain acquired from his Dutch satellite key territories on the route to India, Ceylon and the Cape of Good Hope. A renowned 1805 cartoon by Gillray summed up the situation: Bonaparte and Pitt face each other over a plum-pudding globe, the former slicing away at Europe with his sword, the latter carving himself a huge portion of the world.

Thomas Jefferson said that America's conquest of Canada would be a "mere matter of marching". But its attempted invasion during the 1812-14

A cutting satire in every sense, this cartoon by James Gillray (1756-1815) contrasts Britain's imperial capacities with those of its manic and malignant arch-enemy, Little Boney.

war, which had been prompted by the Royal Navy's vigorous assertion of its sovereignty of the seas, was humiliatingly rebuffed. British forces not only burned Washington but, before torching President Madison's residence (subsequently, of course, resurrected as the White House), drank his "super-excellent Madeira" and ate the banquet prepared for his generals, whom one naval officer ironically dubbed those "resolute champions of republican freedom".

In due course Americans found it more profitable to go west rather than north into what most regarded as a frozen wilderness. To grab Canada, as the radical journalist William Cobbett said, would be the act of a thief who should "steal a stone for the pleasure of carrying it about in his pocket". As the American threat receded, however, Canadian solidarity weakened.

Settlers of French descent increasingly suffered from an acute sense of alienation. It was compounded by racial and religious antagonism, cultural and linguistic isolation, and grinding rural poverty. Their discontent was aggravated by the steady influx of Anglophone and Protestant immigrants after 1815, who sometimes caused trouble themselves. The French Canadians, using Jacobin and Yankee slogans, agitated for national independence. Violent disturbances led to an armed uprising in 1837, which was harshly suppressed by British troops. Fearing that Canada would follow the example of the United States, Lord Melbourne appointed the Earl of Durham Governor-General to introduce a healing policy. Durham was vain, arrogant and rich – he once said that anyone should be able to "jog along on £40,000 a year". But he was also a democrat, known as "Radical Jack". His Report, issued in 1839, said that a united, federal Canada should be granted a system of free and responsible government such as would "give the people a real control over its own destinies". This crucial principle left the mother country a measure of direction, notably in foreign affairs. But it opened the way towards complete self-determination and was duly adopted in Britain's other large white colonies of settlement, Australia, New Zealand and South Africa. The Durham Report became the Magna Carta of the Dominions and the *vade mecum* of the Commonwealth.

Durham's proposals were gradually implemented in Canada. They helped to create an Anglo-French community of interest, though hardly a union of hearts, and fostered loyalty to the British crown. In 1867 the Canadian confederation was formed from the nucleus of Ontario, Quebec, New Brunswick and Nova Scotia, with other provinces joining later – Newfoundland, England's first colony, as late as 1949.

To avoid provoking America, which purchased Alaska after the Civil War and was still suspected of wanting to absorb the entire continent, Canada became not a Kingdom but the first British Dominion. Durham had wanted to bind this incipient nation together with blood and iron: state-aided immigration from Britain and transcontinental railroads. Many immigrants, especially from Ireland, did receive assisted passages and land grants. And in 1885 Ontario was linked to British Columbia by a stupendous feat of engineering. As the Commonwealth historian Nicholas Mansergh memorably observed, Canada was "a railway in search of a state".

Efforts to forge that state from settlements thinly scattered across forest, prairie, muskeg and mountain lasted for over half a century. The task was made harder by regional and ethnic differences. In particular the French Canadian quarter of the population (which numbered eight million by 1914) felt that its existence depended on resisting national integration. The schism was exacerbated by anti-Popery Ulstermen, dour Puritans who, according to jests of the time, kept the Sabbath and anything else they could lay their hands on, and made it possible for visitors to spend a week in Toronto on a Sunday. The cleavage deepened over the question of supporting Britain in war, first against the Boers and then against the Germans.

Loyalists flocked to the colours in 1914 but most French Canadians opposed enlistment and abominated conscription. Some, however, hoped to maintain a dualistic Dominion by fighting for the imperial cause and it proved possible to avert a terminal discord between the *Marseillaise* and *Rule Britannia*. By 1918 sixty thousand Canadians had been killed, many in heroic engagements such as the assault on Vimy Ridge. Their sacrifice was honoured in the Ottawa war memorial, which features a representative group of bronze combatants passing through a granite arch symbolising the portal of nationhood. As a result of the Great War Canada became a sovereign state, while still owing allegiance to the crown. Indeed, in the crucible of conflict all the dominions were transmuted, according to a formula coined by Canadian Prime Minister Robert Borden, into "autonomous nations of an Imperial Commonwealth".

Captain James Cook, painted by Nathaniel Dance in 1776

Chapter Four

ANTIPODES

The first Governor of New South Wales, Captain Arthur Phillip, visualised that Australia could become "the Empire of the East". But he wanted free settlers, not convicts, to lay its foundation. This was understandable since few of those transported had the skills necessary to build a successful community. Most of them were young working men found guilty of minor offences such as theft and they at once proved intractable subjects. When the 200 female felons joined the 600 males at Sydney Cove on 6 February 1788 rogue coupled with whore, according to one convict, in a wild "scene of debauchery and riot". The orgy was overtaken by a violent thunderstorm, whereupon the first inmates of the penal colony under the Southern Cross shook their fists at the sky and cursed their fate. Before transportation ceased completely eighty years later some 165,000 convicts had been sent to Australia, over a tenth of them Irish with no love for John Bull.

Although a benevolent despot, Phillip imposed a punitive regime. Its aim was to ensure that Australia was a penitentiary not a sunny haven where promiscuous delinquents were, as one English critic wrote, "filled every day with rum and kangaroo". Convicts who reverted to crime or tried to escape were flogged or hanged. Those averse to work were consigned to chain gangs. Hellish satellite colonies for incorrigibles were established in Tasmania and

Group of Natives of Tasmania. Painting by Robert Dowling in 1859

Norfolk Island. The inmates of this Antipodean gaol proved unamenable to discipline and their toughness was further tested by the initial struggle for survival. The Sydney soil was barren and prone to drought, rations were cut, some felons died of starvation and food supplies remained precarious for twenty years. To promote cultivation Phillip emancipated some convicts and gave them land. One such, George Barrington, known as the Prince of Pickpockets (and transported to a country where, it was wryly observed, the natives had no pockets to pick), was soon appointed chief constable of Parramatta.

Phillip also begged Pitt's government to send him "a few honest, intelligent settlers". They began to arrive in the 1790s, attracted by free passages, by grants of land, seed, tools and livestock, and by convict labour. By 1820, when the authoritarian Governor Lachlan Macquarie had tidied up the mess left by Phillip's unworthy successors and made striking improvements in many directions, free settlers were in the majority. Macquarie's policy was to create a single Australian flock from these voluntary immigrants, known as "pure merinos", and unshackled felons, erstwhile black sheep. He was attacked for trying to make colonial citizens from social outcasts, "debased, burglarious, brutified, larcenous and pick-pocketous". But Macquarie insisted that meritorious emancipists deserved a stake in the country. And progressive Australians increasingly aspired to enjoy the full rights of Englishmen.

Of course there was no question of extending rights of any kind to the Aboriginal people. On the contrary, in Australia as in the other dominions

'The Founding of Australia by Capt. Arthur Phillip R.N.' (Sydney Cove, Jan. 26th 1788). Painted by Algernon Talmage in 1937

and elsewhere in the Empire, the British incursion had a fatal impact on the indigenous population. Mainly this was because there was no local resistance to European diseases: within a short time, for example, some half of the Aborigines around Sydney succumbed to smallpox. But the colonists were also determined that "savages" should make way for "civilisation", an attitude reinforced by crude reference to Charles Darwin's principle of survival of the fittest. The extermination of native races might thus be seen as part of a benign evolutionary process, and an imperialist such as Winwood Reade could declare: "The law of murder is the law of growth."

In Tasmania the Aboriginal inhabitants were virtually wiped out in the one evident genocide of the British Empire. In Australia they were hunted, killed, dispossessed, degraded and demoralised. Between 1788 and 1900 the Aboriginal population declined drastically, perhaps by as much as eighty per cent.

During the 1850s, by contrast, the white population tripled, to just over a million. This was mainly a result of the discovery of gold and the abundance of "golden fleece" – with twenty sheep per person Australia became the largest wool producer in the world. Australians could thus afford the elected assemblies they demanded and by 1860 all but one of the colonies had achieved a degree of self-government. Forty years later, as foreshadowed by the Durham Report, the separate states combined to form the Commonwealth of Australia. This confederation reflected a hunger for freedom that went back to convict days and now took the form of a desire for self-determination. The Australian character had always been imbued with a spirit of independence and radicals expressed their resentment at the tutelage of the mother country by scorning the "Union Jackals" and the "British Vampire". The Sydney *Bulletin* dubbed it "a nigger empire, run by Jews". Nevertheless most Australians remained fiercely loyal to Britain, as they showed during the Boer War and still more the Great War.

The blood shed by Australian (and New Zealand – ANZAC) forces at Gallipoli was the seed of an Antipodean creation myth. Thus the Diggers, ill-led by effete British commanders but united in the mateship of the bush and treating shrapnel like a summer shower, engendered a new national consciousness. Australia was born again through the sacrifice of its finest sons.

There is some truth in this. The gnomish Australian Prime Minister Billy Hughes established his country as a British ally, not an auxiliary, and insisted that it should speak for itself at the Versailles Peace Conference. Like the other dominions, moreover, Australia gained (by the 1931 Statute of Westminster) legal autonomy and equality of status within the Commonwealth. Thanks to Anzac valour, said Hughes, Australians had "put on the toga of manhood".

On the other hand, Gallipoli and the more terrible Anzac suffering in France also strengthened imperial patriotism in Australia. Anzac Day was a festival of Empire. Australians still regarded themselves as true Britons. So deep was their devotion to the Motherland that Australia and New Zealand mobilised once again to resist Hitler.

White New Zealanders were always keen to identify with their august parent on the other side of the globe if only to distinguish themselves from their felonious neighbour across the Tasman Sea. They prided themselves on forming a "gentleman's colony", the "Britain of the South". Indeed, they traced their country's origins back to the missionary work of Samuel Marsden, who began preaching to the Maoris on Christmas Day 1814, and to the colonising endeavour of Edward Gibbon Wakefield, who promoted the dispatch of 1,200 settlers to New Zealand in 1839. Lord Durham himself supported this enterprise, claiming that its object was "the civilisation of a savage people and the acquirement of a fine field for the employment of British industry". Victorian visitors were equally positive, declaring that immigrants of good stock were transforming a subtropical wilderness into an English country garden, right down to the imported rooks cawing in Christchurch Cathedral close.

In fact the antecedents of New Zealand were by no means wholly respectable. The first whites to tread its shores included whalers, sealers, traders, beachcombers, deserters and escaped convicts. They clashed repeatedly with the warlike natives, enslaving their men, debauching their women and trafficking in tattooed Maori heads. Marsden damned them as "devil's missionaries" though they were indeed leavened by Christian missionaries, who arrived in numbers. These spread the Gospel, the Maoris' first printed literature, into this "land of cannibalism" – actually its people found European flesh too salty for their taste. Maoris were quick to learn, to read and to convert. But they suspected that the colonists for Christ, who undermined their culture and who explained the sharp decline in their numbers (mainly from disease) as a divine visitation, had come to sanctify their extinction. And they would find a further use for pages of the Bible as gun-wadding.

Wakefield's emigration scheme made further conflict inevitable. It involved the "purchase" from the Maoris of 20 million acres for goods worth under £9,000, including twelve shaving brushes and sixty red night caps. Lord Melbourne's government was reluctant to intervene; but since settlers could not be prevented from going to the Antipodes it felt bound to protect them from the natives and vice versa. So in 1840 Britain annexed New Zealand. Here was another proof, said Melbourne, of "the fatal necessity by which a

nation that once begins to colonise is led step by step over the whole globe". The crown's title to the country was established in the same year by the Treaty of Waitangi (Water of Weeping), signed by over 500 Maori chiefs.

But this document was hopelessly ambiguous. The British believed that they had gained sovereignty while bestowing civilisation; the Maoris thought that they had conceded vague overlordship in return for territorial security. In practice the settlers ousted the natives from prime land. This resulted in a series of Maori Wars between 1845 and 1872, during which thousands of British troops ensured, with much difficulty, that the march of civilisation was not impeded by "a handful of savages".

During this time Europeans began to outnumber Maoris, thanks largely to a gold rush. Most of the settlers were working-class Britons – Charles Darwin called them "the very refuse of society". Many came from Scotland and Ireland, whose people played a disproportionately large role in all imperial affairs. But they considered their colony to be "the cream of the British Empire" and were vehemently "John-Bullish". Achieving self-government in the 1850s, they got adult suffrage by 1893. Refusing to join the Australian Confederation, they formed an independent Dominion in 1907. Unlike Canada and Australia (and Ireland), New Zealand embraced conscription during the First World War, sending a tenth of its 1.1 million inhabitants to serve the Empire. Like the other Dominions, it came of age as a nation during the conflict; yet the Kiwis still swore by imperial loyalty. The war memorial on Brooklyn Hill overlooking Wellington expressed a typical sentiment: THE MOTHERLAND CALLED AND THEY WENT. Beneath this inscription, heading a list of 48 names, came the words: AND THESE MEN DIED FOR THEIR COUNTRY.

The last four Tasmanian Aborigines of solely indigenous descent circa 1860.
Truganini, seated far right, was the last to survive.

Chapter Five

CAPE CONFLICTS

South Africa became the Empire's fourth great "white" dominion. But it was not only the home of an extensive and variegated African population but of two mutually hostile European tribes, the British and the Boers. The latter were Dutch farmers, whose Calvinist forebears had come to Cape in the 17th and 18th centuries. Reliant on the Bible and the rifle, they had staked a brutal claim to increasing amounts of territory. This was annexed by the British in 1815 as a strategic and commercial stronghold. Lord Liverpool's government assisted the emigration of British settlers, five thousand of whom landed at Algoa Bay in 1820. Afrikaners resented colonial rule, particularly the more liberal approach to race relations exemplified by the emancipation of slaves in 1833. During that decade 15,000 Boers (over a third of the total) ventured into the interior to preserve their own freedom to impose white mastery. The Great Trek became, in Afrikaner mythology, the exodus of a new chosen people in search of the Promised Land.

This brought the Boers into vicious conflict with the most formidable native warriors in South Africa, the Zulus. Anxious to keep the peace and to secure the port of Durban, Britain appropriated Natal in 1843. The Boers retreated northwards and established their independence in the Transvaal and the Orange Free State. But these republics were poor and weak. By 1877 the

The battle of Isandlwana. A British officer is attacked by Zulu warriors. Painting by Charles Edwin Fripp (1854-1906)

Transvaal only had 12s 6d in its exchequer and the Postmaster General was paid his salary in stamps. When menaced by the Zulu King, Cetshwayo, it submitted to British annexation. Thereupon Sir Bartle Frere, High Commissioner in Cape Town, shut his ears to pacific pleas from London and set out to crush the Zulus, whom he described as "magnificent animals" but "quite out of hand".

What followed was one of the greatest disasters in imperial history: the battle of Isandlwana, at which Cetshwayo's impis cut the British invasion force to pieces. It was, however, a Pyrrhic victory and by 1879 breech-loading Martini-Henrys had triumphed over stabbing assegais. The Afrikaner leader, Paul Kruger, took the opportunity to repudiate Queen Victoria's rule, which led to an outbreak of hostilities in 1880. Once again the British army suffered a humiliating defeat, at Majuba Hill. W. E. Gladstone's government relinquished the Transvaal, retaining only an ambiguous "suzerainty" and boxing in the Boers by seizing Bechuanaland. But in 1886 gold was discovered on the Witwatersrand, a reef so rich as to outshine the diamond deposits of Kimberley. The Transvaal became Eldorado.

Kruger aimed to use its wealth to secure its autonomy but this policy was undermined by the influx of *Uitlanders* (foreigners, mostly Britons) dazzled by the prospect of finding Johannesburg's streets paved with gold. Furthermore

Kruger was challenged by that most formidable of British empire-builders, Cecil Rhodes. Rhodes had made a fortune from diamonds and in 1890 he became Prime Minister of the Cape Colony, which (along with Natal) had enjoyed self-government since 1872. He envisioned the creation of a Greater Britain that would dominate the globe and he expressed a wish to annex the planets if possible – whereas Kruger, like an Old Testament prophet, once assured the circumnavigator Joshua Slocum that the earth was flat.

Rhodes's key venture was the invasion, disguised as a private mining expedition, of the territory that afterwards bore his name, Rhodesia. In 1893 his friend, doctor and agent, Leander Starr Jameson, mowed down the Matabele with machine-guns and established his headquarters in Bulawayo, its first hotel being called "The Maxim". Rhodes, himself nicknamed the Colossus, now aimed to form a British confederation stretching from Cape to Congo, perhaps to Cairo. Kruger stood in his way.

Rhodes plotted to topple him, using the *Uitlanders* as his pretext and instrument. They outnumbered the Boers and paid nearly all the Transvaal's taxes, yet Kruger denied them the vote. Rhodes won the secret support of Joseph Chamberlain, the powerful Colonial Secretary, whose dreams of consolidating the Empire matched his own.

But the 1895 coup, known as the Jameson Raid, was woefully mismanaged. The *Uitlanders* failed to rise. Boer forces stalked Jameson's motley private army all the way from Bechuanaland. And after a brief clash near Johannesburg it surrendered. Kruger sent the ringleaders for trial in London, where Jameson was imprisoned. He was also feted and saluted in Kipling's poem *If*. Manfully he perjured himself at the parliamentary committee of inquiry, known as "the Lying in State at Westminster". Chamberlain was exonerated but Rhodes had to resign. This ignominious episode hardened British-Boer antagonism and Kruger purchased Mauser rifles and ammunition from Germany. Asked why he required such an arsenal, he replied: "Oh, Kaffirs, Kaffirs – and such-like objects."

In 1897 Chamberlain appointed Sir Alfred Milner South African High Commissioner. It was, this militant visionary told the Colonial Secretary, "a *fighting post*". Although half-German, Milner was a "British Race Patriot" and he believed imperialism to be "the highest development of patriotism". The Boers, he thought, should be subordinated, either by being made to enfranchise the *Uitlanders*, or, if necessary, by force. Milner was no Midas. Gold for him was power in ingot form and it was territorial power that he (and Chamberlain and the Prime Minister, Lord Salisbury) craved. This Kruger tearfully recognised: "It is our country you want."

He therefore struck first, in 1899, hoping to occupy Natal before imperial reinforcements arrived and to draw on international support, especially from Germany. This did not materialise and the invasion stalled. But the sharp-shooting frontiersmen of the veldt were the finest armed horsemen since the Mongols. Skilfully led by the likes of Jan Smuts and Luis Botha, they received untoward assistance from the enemy, whose astonishingly inept commanders suffered a series of traumatic reverses early in the war. Not for the first or the last time, British soldiers were said to be lions led by donkeys.

Eventually imperial strength told. A quarter of a million troops drove the

Cetshwayo kaMpande, king of the Zulu from 1873 to 1879. Photograph by Alexander Bassanno

CECIL RHODES 1853-1902

Cecil Rhodes saw himself as a modern Caesar and the British Empire, during its expansionist heyday, had no more ardent champion. Believing in the innate superiority of the Anglo-Saxon race, he aspired to bring "the whole uncivilised world under British rule". And he anticipated that the ascendancy of the English-speaking peoples, including Americans, would usher in a reign of universal peace. Having made a fortune in South Africa, Rhodes attempted to realise his imperial vision. In the process he gave his name to two great countries – now Zimbabwe and Zambia. When Rhodes stood on the Cape, wrote Mark Twain, "his shadow falls to the Zambezi". Others said that it extended to the Nile and darkened the globe.

Rhodes was born in Bishop's Stortford, the fifth son of an Anglican clergyman. A sickly youth, he was sent off at the age of seventeen to make good in the colonies. After growing cotton in Natal, he garnered a far richer harvest from the recently discovered diamond fields of Kimberley. By means of ingenuity, cajolery and bribery, he amalgamated rival concerns into De Beers Mining Company, which exercised stringent control over African labour and virtually monopolised the supply of gems. He himself was interested in imperial rather than financial dividends. King of diamonds Rhodes might be, but he regarded such wealth as crystallised power. It was power he deployed with unscrupulous cynicism, maintaining that every man had his price and that the ends justified the means.

Entering politics, Rhodes set out to create a British United States of Africa. Bechuanaland was seized in 1884 to hem in the Boer Republics, which threatened British hegemony thanks to gold strikes on the Witwatersrand. Rhodes wrung mining concessions from African chiefs and used them as a pretext to occupy Mashonaland in 1890, when he became Prime Minister of Cape Colony.

In 1893, on similar grounds, he invaded Matabeleland, slaughtering King Lobengula's warriors with Maxim guns which, as Hilaire Belloc wrote, we had got and they had not. Rhodes congratulated himself on this economical form of warfare, imposed a punitive regime and crushed a subsequent revolt with the utmost ferocity. The Colossus assured white settlers that their destiny was to rule Rhodesia.

In 1895, however, Rhodes was forced to resign when the Jameson Raid, the insurrection he plotted against the Transvaal government, proved an abject failure. He continued to campaign for British supremacy in South Africa, a goal achieved at huge cost by the Boer War. Rhodes died just before it ended, his famous last words being "So much to do, so little done!" Among his bequests were the scholarships that bear his name, a name that provokes controversy to this day.

Above: Sketch of Cecil Rhodes by Violet Manners

The Colossus. Punch printed this cartoon (10 December 1892) after Rhodes announced plans for a telegraph line and a railroad linking the Cape to Cairo.

Afrikaners back and relieved the besieged towns of Kimberley, Ladysmith and Mafeking – the last greeted with jingoistic exultation in England. But Boer "bitter-enders" resorted to guerrilla warfare, to which the new British commander, Herbert Kitchener, responded by scorching the earth. He built 8,000 blockhouses, erected 3,700 miles of barbed wire, burned 30,000 farms, destroyed crops and killed livestock. Boer families were thus driven into so-called "concentration camps", where 28,000 (a sixth of the Boer population, mostly women and children) died of disease, malnutrition and neglect.

At home Liberals and others condemned such "methods of barbarism". David Lloyd George charged Salisbury with carrying out what was, in effect, "a policy of extermination". At a time when the Empire had never seemed more substantial, Britain's last major war of territorial gain gravely under-mined its moral foundations. It was, too, a prelude to the world wars which fatally sapped the Empire's military and economic might. Kipling described the South African conflict as a "dress-parade for Armageddon".

Kitchener himself urged a peace of reconciliation, which was signed at Vereeniging in 1902. By its terms Afrikaners became subjects of the crown. But the Transvaal and the Orange Free State were promised independ-ence within the Empire, in the hope that the Boers would become loyal imperial subjects. Ultimately this hope was vitiated by searing memories of the Afrikaners' war-time agony. But in the short term the peace, along with an amnesty, reparations and reconstruction, suited both sides. The British did attempt to safeguard the interests of Africans, who had suffered most of all during the war. However, as Milner cynically remarked, to win the game in South Africa "you have only to sacrifice 'the nigger' absolutely".

After the settlement Africans were subjected to discrimination and segregation, conditions paving the way for *apartheid*. As early as 1907 the Liberal government granted the Dutch republics self-rule, not least because it was thus able to shuffle off the responsibility for "Chinese slavery", the punitive employment of indentured labour in the gold mines for which Milner was denounced – Winston Churchill dubbed him the "disconsolate proconsul". Three years later the Union of South Africa was formed, a unitary state with full dominion status. Botha and Smuts took their country to war against Germany in 1914, suppressing a rebellion of "bitter-enders" in the process. They calculated that the best interests of their nation would be served, for the time being at least, by adhering to the largest empire in the world.

Opposite: Horatio Herbert Kitchener, 1st Earl Kitchener (1850–1916)

Chapter Six

EAST OF SUEZ

India was famously the jewel in the British crown. The raj conferred imperial status on Queen Victoria's sprawling realm and enabled her, in 1876, to adopt the title Empress of India. The security of this glittering garrison state, a unique source of power, profit and prestige, was deemed vital to the interests of the British Empire as a whole. The Empire, as Admiral Jackie Fisher said, floated on the Royal Navy, whose task it was to protect the sea lanes to India. These stretched round the globe and were guarded by key bases: Gibraltar, Malta, Aden, the Cape, Trincomalee, Sydney, Singapore and Hong Kong. The last two were of particular importance in another triangular trade which greatly augmented imperial strength after the Napoleonic Wars: Indian opium sold to China covered the cost of Chinese tea imports to Britain, which itself found a market in the subcontinent for textiles and other products of the Industrial Revolution. Thus Britain created in the Orient what has been called the world's first "narco-military" empire, a commercial nexus at the heart of an expanding miscellany of possessions.

Thomas Stamford Raffles was responsible for the foundation of Singapore in 1819. He was a clerk in the East India Company's service who had risen by energy and audacity to take a leading part in the victorious struggle against the Dutch in Asia and to become master of Java. After Waterloo, however,

Portrait of five opium smokers in Eastern Bengal during the 1860s

the Company handed back Java and accepted the revival of Dutch rule in the East Indies, thus obtaining advantages in Malaya and counteracting French influence in Indochina.

Raffles himself condemned Dutch colonialism as brutal and corrupt, not without reason. He claimed that extending British power into the Indonesian archipelago served "the cause of humanity" and he treated natives like an indulgent father – the "Battas are not bad people", he said, "notwithstanding they eat each other". After diligent exploration, Raffles perceived the unique potential of a fishing village set amid mangroves on the island at the tip of the Malay peninsula. It could become a grand commercial entrepôt and a "*fulcrum* whence we may extend our influence politically", he wrote – "what *Malta* is in the West". Singapore did indeed become Lion City (Singa means lion), an apparently impregnable fortress dominating the trade routes of Asia.

Britain had long been eager to open up China to its merchants. But Lord Macartney's mission to Peking in 1793 had been humiliatingly rebuffed amid mutual disdain and incomprehension. Macartney had refused to kow-tow to the Emperor Qianlong, who insisted that he was a barbarian tribute-bearer and declared that the Celestial Empire had not "the slightest need of your country's manufactures". Further overtures had been equally unsuccessful. British traders, known as "foreign devils", were confined to Canton where they had to pay for tea with silver since no other goods were acceptable – not even, as they hoped, tweed. However the British craving for tea was out-matched by the Chinese addiction to opium.

During the 1830s this narcotic was imported from India, with the help of Chinese smugglers, in such quantities that the entire Middle Kingdom seemed in danger of being demoralised and impoverished. In 1839 the Emperor Tao-Kuang took forceful steps to suppress the traffic, which precipitated the First Opium War. Critics declared that fighting on behalf of drug-dealers was a national sin. But the Foreign Secretary Lord Palmerston, an ebullient champion of gunboat diplomacy, determined to teach the Chinese a lesson in what he claimed to be the interests of free trade. This he did with an over-whelming demonstration of British technological superiority, typified by the heavily armed iron paddle steamer *Nemesis* – the Chinese tried to copy it with a ship powered by coolies on a treadmill. By the Treaty of Nanking (1842), Britain extorted a variety of commercial concessions, notably sovereignty over Hong Kong. The island was described as a kind of bonded warehouse for the opium trade.

The Chinese continued to be obstructive and so Palmerston, Prime Minister by 1860, seized the opportunity to give them another "exemplary drub-bing". The Second Opium War culminated in the looting and burning of the Emperor's Summer Palace outside Peking, an act of vandalism which outraged European opinion though Palmerston was "quite enchanted" by it. Among the plunder Queen Victoria received a Pekinese dog, sacred to royalty, which was christened Looty.

China was forced to legalise the opium traffic and open itself to foreign-ers, who established small, quasi-colonial settlements in so-called "treaty ports", notably Shanghai. Some Britons nursed ambitions to oust the Son of Heaven from the Dragon Throne and to turn his decaying realm into a second India, a yellow raj. But Palmerston did not want to incur further military and administrative burdens. Sufficient unto the day was commercial exploitation, including the systematic transportation of coolies to work abroad, which was reminiscent of the slave trade. Lenin accused Britain and other imperial pow-ers of robbing China as ghouls rob a corpse.

Chinese resentment burst out with particular ferocity during the Boxer Rising in 1900, when members of a secret society known as the Righteous Harmonious Fists revolted against the unbearable alien intrusion. The Boxers were defeated but the vulnerability of the micro-colonies clinging to the vast epidermis of China had been demonstrated. In Hong Kong the British relaxed their harsher forms of paternalistic regulation, such as pass laws. India officially ceased to sell opium to China in 1913 but Governors of Hong Kong dragged their feet because the drug still supplied half the colony's revenue. It was, however, gradually phased out between the world wars. During that time Hong Kong lapsed into a colonial torpor of its own, succumbing to what Churchill once called "the fatal lassitude of the Orient". Failing to mobilise Chinese manpower, it became an easy victim of Japanese aggression in 1941. The fall of Hong Kong, though much less earth-shaking than that of Singapore, was a terrible revelation of Britain's imperial weakness east of Suez.

Burma was especially difficult to control. To protect India and exploit rich natural resources such as teak and rubies, the British engorged this diversified realm in three stages, culminating in the deposition of King Thibaw in 1885. He had dominated every sphere of Burmese life and his removal filled his subjects with lasting fury against the invaders. It took British forces five years of vicious fighting to crush opposition and thereafter even boys in paddy-fields would chant: "It is not fit that foreigners should rule the royal Golden Land."

Viceroys of India regarded Burma not so much as a province of the raj as a cockpit of rebellion. Thus British rule, though not without its benefits, was oppressive. Even by the 1930s, when the population was under 17 million, a hundred hangings took place each year, their horror being starkly evoked in a celebrated essay by George Orwell. Racial and religious grievances festered, particularly over the import of Indian labour, and Buddhist monks spearheaded nationalist agitation. One Burmese leader, Ba Maw, declared: "Our first task is to get rid of the ogre riding on our backs."

To maintain its ascendancy Britain made concessions. The Government of India Act (1935) established a parliament in Rangoon, giving Burma a large measure of self-rule within the Empire. But the Governor still had the whip hand. As the Japanese menace grew, Ba Maw and the revolutionary Aung San (father of Aung San Suu Kyi) formed a Freedom Bloc. It surreptitiously looked eastwards for assistance. Asked by the Labour politician Stafford Cripps in 1940 what the Burmese would do, Ba Maw replied: "The Burmese will act in the Burmese way." Cripps persisted: "What is the Burmese way?" Ba Ma answered: "That's a Burmese secret." The Freedom Bloc's leaders were arrested, though Aung San escaped to Japan.

In 1941 the new Prime Minister, U Saw, came to England with an offer of Burmese support against Nippon in return for a guarantee of full independence. Churchill approved the visit provided that, he told Leo Amery, Secretary of State for India and Burma, "you see U Saw". Nothing came of it. But on his return journey U Saw flew over Pearl Harbour the day after it was bombed and at once made overtures to Tokyo. Such was the gravitational pull exerted on Britain's oriental colonies by the Land of the Rising Sun.

Ceylon, whose inhabitants preferred collaboration to confrontation with imperial overlords, was idealised as "the pearl drop on the brow of India". The British had completed their mastery of the island by subjugating the Kandyan kingdom in 1818, when some ten thousand people were killed, one per cent of the total population. Thereafter few disturbances occurred, though the influx of Tamils, brought in to work on the coffee and tea plantations, stored up trouble for the future. The Navy commanded the Indian Ocean from its magnificent natural harbour at Trincomalee. British rule ashore was authoritarian but, as Leonard Woolf observed, 1906 Ceylon was "the exact opposite of a 'police state'". To illustrate the point Woolf described how he and a couple of other imperial officers supervised the pearl fisheries south of Adam's Bridge, which attracted 30,000 people from all over Asia, armed with nothing more lethal than walking sticks.

The Ceylonese elite aspired not to beat the British but to join them, to speak English, play cricket and imitate Western ways. However, these included the establishment of democratic freedoms which, nationalists said, accorded with the dignity of Ceylon's ancient race and rich cultural heritage. The future Prime Minister, S. W. R. D. Bandaranaike, compared its colonised natives to animals in a zoo, unaware of their captivity.

They certainly profited little from alien rule. Although the British built roads, railways and canals, reviving the archaic irrigation system, ninety per cent of the population lived in rural poverty. But the polite pressure of the educated few, who formed the Ceylon National Congress in 1919, persuaded the Colonial Office to sanction a revolutionary degree of autonomy. In 1931 Ceylon became the first Asian and colonial country to elect a State Council by universal suffrage. The Governor retained control over justice, finance, defence and foreign policy but Ceylonese ministers were given charge of such departments as health, education, transport and agriculture.

Many whites were appalled, insisting that brown-skinned people should be treated as children, from whom subservience was expected – one planter smashed an official's umbrella because "it was impudent for a native to carry one in the face of a European". But the new ministers, notably D. S. Senanayake, who was a keen cricketer and an ardent sportsman in the English mould, demonstrated that Europeans had no monopoly in the art of government.

Sir Thomas Stamford Raffles, 1781–1826

Ceylon was ripe for complete independence, which it gained as a result of its support for the Empire during the Second World War.

Elsewhere the red colouration signifying British hegemony seeped over the map of Asia and into the Pacific. Usually its progress was determined by the wish to secure existing positions or to establish some new strategic or commercial foothold. From their early trading-post in Penang, for example, the British gradually spread their authority over Malaya, colonial residents or advisers becoming the powers behind the sultans' thrones. Siam itself, though never occupied, was tinged with the British influence.

Sometimes the ruddy hue was applied by adventurers such as James Brooke who, in the spirit of Raffles, imposed order on pirate-ravaged North Borneo for the Sultan of Brunei and in 1841 became hereditary Rajah of Sarawak.

Often freelance encroachments provoked trouble and London had to accept the pleas of faraway functionaries that extending the Empire was the only means of safeguarding British interests. Some threats were remote: Lord Salisbury complained about soldiers who were intent on "garrisoning the Moon in order to protect us from Mars".

In 1874, however, there was serious unrest in Fiji, where "blackbirding" (kidnapping workers) was rife. This justified Commodore Goodenough in exceeding his orders and annexing the islands. Disraeli bowed to the tyranny of distance and accepted the *fait accompli*. He assured Queen Victoria, who was horrified by the prospect of having cannibals for subjects, that the Fijians were all Methodists. Equally misleading were the cartographical swathes of red flowing from the United Kingdom, whose size was exaggerated thanks to Mercator's projection.* They gave no clue as to the fragility of the British Empire, particularly in the East.

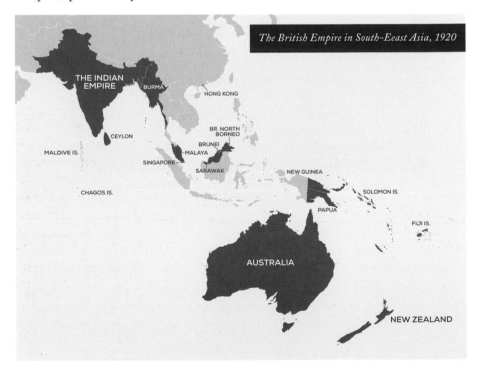

The British Empire in South-Eeast Asia, 1920

THE INDIAN EMPIRE
BURMA
HONG KONG
CEYLON
BR. NORTH BORNEO
BRUNEI
MALDIVE IS.
MALAYA
SINGAPORE
SARAWAK
NEW GUINEA
CHAGOS IS.
SOLOMON IS.
PAPUA
FIJI IS.
AUSTRALIA
NEW ZEALAND

---

* Gerardus Mercator was a Flemish geographer whose map projection in 1569 distorted some areas of the world.

Chapter Seven

SCRAMBLE FOR AFRICA

During the second half of Queen Victoria's reign Britain faced growing challenges to its global pre-eminence. The fortuitous advantage of being the first industrial nation was eroded as other countries began to catch up. America undertook dynamic reconstruction after the Civil War. A unified Germany emerged as a serious competitor. And like Germany, France and other European countries wanted a place in the sun.

Africa, of which only ten per cent was colonised by the 1870s, became a particular focus for their rivalry. The so-called Dark Continent had little but ivory and palm oil to offer in the way of trade, but the great powers were soon as much intent on territorial aggrandisement as on commercial advantage. Thus began what became known as the scramble for Africa. Britain conducted an aggressive defence.

Its first move occurred as a result of the opening of the Suez Canal in 1869. This was a Franco-Egyptian enterprise and British governments had been slow to appreciate the significance of the waterway, which provided the shortest sea route to India. Benjamin Disraeli made up for the mistake. In 1875 he acquired the shares of the bankrupt Egyptian ruler Khedive Ismail in the company that owned the Canal, telling Queen Victoria: "You have it, Madam." The Suez Canal was at once seen as the jugular vein of the Empire and it engaged Britain closely in the affairs of Egypt, a failing state owing nominal allegiance to Turkey, supposedly "the sick man of Europe". Prompted by resentment at foreign interference, a nationalist revolt led by Colonel Ahmed Arabi broke out in 1882. Gladstone was reluctantly persuaded to restore stability in Egypt and thus to protect the Canal, a feat accomplished by General Wolseley in what he called the "tidiest little war" ever fought by a British army.

As a Liberal Gladstone disparaged aggressive Tory imperialism; but he by no means disavowed the Empire when he could convince himself – and critics said he could convince himself of anything – that it was a force for good. So while promising to let the Egyptian people go he began a process of turning their country into a "veiled protectorate". Thus what started as a temporary occupation lasted until another Suez crisis blew up seventy-four years later. Meanwhile Britain became embroiled in Egypt's vast Sudanese dependency. This was in the grip of a rebellion led by a self-proclaimed messiah called the

'General Gordon's Last Stand' by George W. Joy

Mahdi. In 1884 General Charles Gordon was sent to withdraw the Egyptian garrison from Khartoum but once there he resolved to hold the city and smash the Mahdi. His telegrams home convinced Gladstone's government that Gordon was a "Christian lunatic" but he was soon being hailed as an imperial martyr. His heroic defence of Khartoum and his death (dramatised in a talismanic painting by George Joy) two days before the arrival of the relief expedition, became one of the epics of the British Empire.

Gladstone was happy to extricate himself from the Sudan and he had no wish to become involved still further south. But tropical Africa had gradually been reconnoitred, the blanks on the map filled by pioneers of different kinds. There were explorers such as Mungo Park, whose best guide to the Niger at the end of the eighteenth century was Herodotus, and John Hanning Speke, who "discovered" the main source of the Nile in 1858. There were missionaries such as David Livingstone, who traced the course of the Zambezi and crusaded against slavery, "this open sore of the world" which could only be healed, he said, by a new trinity: Christianity, commerce and colonisation. There were soldiers such as Sir Robert Napier, who in 1868 upheld British honour in Ethiopia by sacking Magdala, stronghold of the Emperor Theodore – he shot himself with a silver pistol that had been presented to him on behalf of Queen Victoria.

Hunters, adventurers, traders, naturalists, prospectors and other harbingers of empire pushed out the frontiers of knowledge and opened up new spheres of British influence in Africa where the gospel could be preached, the market established and the flag raised. In 1884, taking advantage of Gladstone's preoccupation with Egypt, Germany's Iron Chancellor, Otto von Bismarck, established a protectorate over South West Africa.

This unexpected move was a precursor to further grabs for Africa by European nations which were now keen to augment their prestige by colonial means. Gladstone, having initially said that Bismarck was welcome to his "sterile sand hole", made Bechuanaland a protectorate in 1885. This set a limit to German (and Boer) expansion in the region and it was designed to safeguard existing imperial interests. In fact the British scramble for tropical Africa was intended to establish bastions, ramparts and outworks, however remote, to protect the two key strategic points on the continent, Suez and the Cape. Lord Salisbury, who succeeded Gladstone, also hoped the partition of Africa might help to maintain the balance of power, and thus keep the peace, in Europe. Salisbury joked that its rulers were competing for tracts of central Africa which they could neither pronounce nor locate. But he ensured that Britain got the lion's share, 2.5 million square miles. Included were territories in what can conveniently be called Nigeria (1885), Somaliland (1888), Rhodesia (1889), Nyasaland (1891), Uganda (1894), Kenya (1895), the Gold Coast (1896) and the Sudan (1898).

British colonisation of Africa was piecemeal, spasmodic and incoherent. It took different forms and employed a variety of methods, ranging from persuasion and collaboration to fraud and force. Above all, it was cheese-paring, conducted with a careful eye to costs and benefits. This explains why so much of British expansion was carried out by private enterprise and led by freelance empire-builders. Thus Sir George Goldie's Royal Niger Company was granted a charter in 1886 to administer the delta region and pushed north ruthlessly, though he refused to name the occupied territory, taken over by the crown in 1899, Goldesia. Harry Johnston, subsidised by Rhodes's South Africa Company and supported by a few Sikh troops, gained Nyasaland for the Empire, securing treaties with headmen where possible, burning native villages where necessary. In 1888 Sir William Mackinnon's Imperial East Africa Company was chartered to promote British interests in this region and only when it failed was a protectorate established. The first commissioner sanctioned British expropriation of Kikuyu land, saying: "These people must learn submission by bullets – it's the only school."

There were, of course, high-minded justifications for painting the African map red, not all of them humbug. Joseph Chamberlain explained the war against the Ashanti in 1895 by saying that it was a national duty to establish the *Pax Britannica* over "savage countries" for the sake of the benighted people themselves. Frederick Lugard, Goldie's most effective agent, declared that he and his ilk were "bringing to the dark places of the earth, the abode of barbarism and cruelty, the torch of culture and progress, while ministering to the material needs of our own civilisation".

Lugard was the champion of a form of indirect rule known as the "dual mandate", whereby the British shared their authority with local chiefs. This system, adopted elsewhere, did not work well and sometimes hardly worked at all, but it compensated for the fact that British officialdom was so thin on the ground. As it was Lugard also ruled directly, employing the whip and the punitive expedition. At the Colonial Office Churchill remarked ironically that Lugard's so-called "pacification" of northern Nigeria was "liable to be misrepresented by persons unacquainted with imperial terminology as the murdering of natives and stealing their lands."

As a young subaltern Churchill had himself witnessed some of the cruelties of empire, notably at Omdurman in 1898. Here Kitchener's army avenged Gordon by mowing down 11,000 Dervishes with rifles, machine-guns and

General Charles Gordon wearing Egyptian uniform in the Sudan in about 1872

DAVID LIVINGSTONE 1813-1873

Victorians regarded David Livingstone as an imperial saint who brought light to the "Dark Continent". And there did indeed seem to be something superhuman about his life-long struggle against almost impossible odds. Born in a one-room tenement outside Glasgow, he was sent to work in a cotton mill at the age of ten, spending twelve hours a day tying up broken threads on spinning jennies. He nevertheless scratched together an education and, sustained by faith that he was God's chosen instrument, he was ordained as a Congregationalist minister and qualified as a medical missionary. In 1840 he took Africa as his parish and came to believe that Britain could introduce it to a golden age.

Determined to preach the Word in virgin territory, he ventured north from the Cape into an interior that was largely uncharted, filled with hazards and blighted by the slave trade. Despite Livingstone's terrific exertions, his missionary journeys were far from successful. He converted only one African, who subsequently lapsed. His remedies hardly improved on those of local witchdoctors. Obstinate and cantankerous, he quarrelled with colleagues. Having

married in 1845, he sacrificed his family to his explorations, during which he relied on others, ultimately on Arab slave traders. While insisting that the Negro should be treated not just as a man and a brother but as a "thorough gentleman", he sometimes flogged his porters. Furthermore his geographical theories were unsound. He tried to prove, for example, that rivers such as the cataract-choked, fever-ridden Zambezi were God's highway into the heart of darkness.

Nevertheless as the standard-bearer of Britain's civilising mission, Livingstone was without peer. Sympathetically presented in his Missionary Travels (1857), his epic criss-crossings of the continent, during which he "discovered" and christened the Victoria Falls, caught the public imagination. Equally appealing were his threefold means of redeeming savage Africa: spreading the Gospel, fostering legitimate commerce, and planting the Union Jack. Only the British Empire, combining moral rectitude with economic and military power, could rid Africa of the scourge of slavery.

Mystery added to the veneration felt for Livingstone during his last, suicidal wanderings, when he disappeared from view in central Africa. In 1871 he was found near Lake Tanganyika by the journalist Henry Morton Stanley, who uttered the immortal words, which embarrassed him to the end of his days: "Dr Livingstone, I presume." Stanley hero-worshipped Livingstone, asserting that he was as nearly angelic as the fallen condition of humanity allowed. When Livingstone died his African retainers returned his embalmed body to England. He was buried in Westminster Abbey, there to enshrine all the zeal and nobility of Britain's imperial enterprise.

Above: David Livingstone in 1864

*An artist's impression of the meeting between David Livingstone and
Henry Morton Stanley*

artillery. To Churchill's horror many of the wounded were either shot or left to die on the battlefield. Kitchener added insult to injury by destroying the Mahdi's tomb, throwing his remains in the Nile and considering whether to make a goblet or a paperweight out of his shapely skull.

There were protests about the slaughter and the desecration, and Kitchener later claimed that he had dispatched the skull in a kerosene tin for burial in the Sudan, though Churchill said that the tin might have contained anything, perhaps ham sandwiches. Nevertheless, Kitchener was hailed as one of the titans of the British Empire, not least for having outfaced the French at Fashoda, where an expedition led by Major Marchand was obliged to withdraw. This facilitated the establishment of an Anglo-Egyptian "condominium" in the Sudan and completed Britain's scramble for Africa.

The British Empire in Africa
and the Middle East, 1920

Chapter Eight

JOHN BULL'S OTHER ISLAND

England had oppressed Ireland ever since the Middle Ages. After the Reformation, the Protestant Ascendancy, with its English Pale around Dublin and its Scottish garrison in Ulster, dominated the Roman Catholic population, which was bound by harsh penal laws during the eighteenth century. Ireland was also subjugated economically, so much so that Jonathan Swift advised his countrymen to burn everything from England but her coal. To quell political dissent Pitt incorporated Ireland into the United Kingdom in 1800, offering Catholic Emancipation (delayed until 1829) as a reward. In theory the merger made Ireland a partner in Britain's imperial enterprise but in practice its impoverished inhabitants were still treated as a vanquished tribe. Irish nationalists regarded the Union as an unbearable extension of the Anglo-Norman yoke and never ceased to struggle, sometimes violently, for its removal. Nothing demonstrated more clearly that Ireland must have the freedom to work out its own salvation than the most terrible tragedy in its history – the Potato Famine.

In 1845 Ireland's population stood at over eight million, a third of whom lived on the brink of starvation. They relied for sustenance on potatoes. Many peasant families, growing them on tiny plots, ate nothing else. When a fungal disease destroyed a quarter of the crop, there was acute distress, alleviated by some government help. But according to laissez-faire orthodoxy, a dole fatally undermined the principle of self-reliance. So in 1846, when the harvest failed almost completely, the British Treasury (itself strapped for cash and for credit) pulled tight the purse strings.

The result was catastrophic, especially in the west, where whole communities became "famished and ghastly skeletons". The Great Hunger, which lasted until 1851 and brought typhus and other diseases in its wake, took a million lives and forced 1.5 million souls to emigrate, mostly to America where they nurtured bitter enmity towards the British Empire.

At the time champions of Irish independence such as Charles Gavan Duffy charged the London government with "a fearful murder committed on the mass of the people". Subsequently there have been claims that the "man-made famine" was an act of "colonial genocide", another Holocaust. It was not that. But the official response was shameful and culpable, reflecting a racist disdain for "Paddy". The English were all too apt to attribute the disaster to Hibernian fecklessness and to blame the potato blight on Popery.

Despite belated English attempts at amelioration, Irish resistance to the Union stiffened after the Famine. It took various forms: Fenian uprisings and terrorist outrages; Gaelic cultural associations; boycotts and protests (sometimes violent) directed against absentee English landlords who rack-rented and evicted their tenants; and an Irish Home Rule party at Westminster which sought, in Gladstone's words, to march "through rapine to the dismemberment of the Empire".

In 1880 Charles Stewart Parnell, a cricketing squire from Wicklow, became its most formidable leader. Even Fenian revolutionaries recognised him as "the man to fight the English; he was so like themselves, cool, callous, inexorable". Parnell created a disciplined parliamentary party and boldly exploited agrarian grievances and disturbances. Gladstone gave ground and then concluded that nothing save independence would pacify Ireland. But his first Home Rule Bill (1886), which prompted Liberal Imperialists such as Joseph Chamberlain to defect to the Tories, was defeated. The new Prime Minister, Lord Salisbury, was haunted by the spectre of imperial disintegration. "Ireland must be kept, like India, at all hazards," he insisted, "by persuasion if possible; if not, by force."

Salisbury's feline nephew (and eventual successor) Arthur Balfour followed this policy. He developed the economy and assisted tenants to buy their holdings; but he also quelled opposition ruthlessly. He built light railways and imposed heavy punishments, earning himself the nickname "Bloody" Balfour. What he failed to appreciate was that Home Rule could not be killed by

The British Lion and the Irish Monkey. A cartoon drawn in April 1848 by John Leech

kindness or by cruelty: there was no substitute for Irish emancipation from English tutelage. Moreover Gladstone's final attempt to satisfy the nationalists (quashed by the House of Lords in 1893) was bedevilled by Protestants in the north, who were existentially wedded to the Union and damned Home Rule as Rome Rule. Politicians at Westminster played the Orange card and Lord Randolph Churchill coined the dangerous slogan, "Ulster will fight and Ulster will be right." By this time Parnell was dead, having been discredited by the exposure of his adulterous affair with Kitty O'Shea. What survived, however, was his most celebrated pronouncement. It was engraved on his Dublin monument and reverberated in hearts all round the British Empire: "No man shall have the right to fix the boundary to the march of a Nation."

Although the Irish parliamentary party was weaker under the leadership of the amiable John Redmond, H. H. Asquith's Liberal government depended on its support after 1910. The following year the Parliament Act restricted the power of the House of Lords to veto legislation and there seemed a chance that Irish independence might be gained by constitutional means. Asquith's Home Rule Bill, however, aroused passionate opposition among Unionists in the north, who formed the Ulster Volunteers, a militia which armed and drilled. They were inspired by the fiery rhetoric of Sir Edward Carson, who had destroyed Oscar Wilde in the witness box, acting, as Wilde said, "with all the added bitterness of an old friend".

Carson in turn was backed by Tories at Westminster and British army officers at the Curragh military base, who contemplated mutiny in the name of loyalty to the crown. The Conservative leader, Bonar Law, told Ulstermen: "you hold the pass for the Empire". As Irish Volunteers mustered in the Catholic south, equipped with smuggled Mauser rifles, civil strife threatened to engulf the island of Ireland. But local hostilities were suspended in August 1914, with the advent of Armageddon.

Redmond pledged Irish support for the English cause during the First World War. But Fenians and their allies, intent on winning freedom by force, took the traditional view that England's difficulty was Ireland's opportunity. The socialist revolutionary James Connolly reckoned that the "Brigand Empire" had never been more vulnerable: Ireland was "in the position of a child that might stick a pin in a giant's heart". So on Easter Monday 1916 some 1,600 Irish Volunteers and others seized key points in Dublin. Outside the General Post Office, the idealistic poet Patrick Pearse proclaimed Ireland a Republic "in the name of God and of the dead generations from which she receives her old tradition of nationhood". It took six days for British troops to crush the rising, which saw the devastation of large parts of the city centre and caused nearly 500 deaths. Dubliners spat at insurgents as they were led away to prison. But the mood changed utterly when the British, determined to show strength and to exact retribution for a war-time stab in the back, shot fifteen of the ringleaders, including Connolly and Pearse. The rebels became martyrs. Their sacrifice was hailed as an act of national redemption. In Yeats's unforgettable words, a terrible beauty was born.

The main beneficiary of the Easter Rising was Sinn Féin (Ourselves), the party most clearly identified with the cause of independence. Its austere leader, Eamon de Valera, routed Redmond's Home Rulers at the polls and in 1919 set up a parliament in Dublin, the Dáil Éirann. Meanwhile Michael Collins established its so-called "military wing", the Irish Republican Army, which initiated guerrilla warfare against the British.

They retaliated with an armed force known, from the colouring of its uniforms, as the Black and Tans. David Lloyd George, Asquith's adroit and unscrupulous successor, encouraged them to grab murder by the throat. But during two years of "troubles", in which 1,500 lives were lost and atrocities occurred on both sides, they alienated not only the Irish population but public opinion around the world. So Lloyd George struck a deal with Collins, whereby Northern Ireland remained within the United Kingdom while in the south an Irish Free State became a self-governing dominion. The treaty split Sinn Féin and precipitated civil war. But in 1937 de Valera made Éire a republic, finally wrenching the harp from the crown. He thus blew a significant hole in the fabric of the British Empire. Churchill called him D'evil Éire.

Chapter Nine

IMPERIAL HIGH NOON

At its zenith in the late-Victorian age, the British Empire bestrode the world like a colossus. Apologists liked to boast that it consisted of "one continent, a hundred peninsulas, five hundred promontories, a thousand lakes, two thousand rivers, ten thousand islands". Greater Britain, its civilising mission sustained by 10,000 overseas missionaries, seemed to be uniquely blessed as the embodiment of might and dominion. Lord Rosebery, who was Prime Minister in 1894-5 and cheered himself up by humming "Rule Britannia", maintained that the Empire was not wholly human since even the most cynical must see in it "the finger of the Divine". At Queen Victoria's Diamond Jubilee in 1897 the *Daily Mail*, a potent new megaphone for imperial monarchy, said it was fitting that the sovereign should pay homage to God at St Paul's because He was the only Being more majestic than she. Adolf Hitler was fascinated by Britain's global hegemony and in *Mein Kampf* he hailed its Empire as "the greatest power on earth".

Hitler later recommended the film *Lives of a Bengal Lancer* to the SS as demonstrating how a tiny elite could subjugate an inferior race; whereas the British preferred to think that in India and elsewhere they were, as Kipling put it, bearing "the White Man's burden". They prided themselves on working for the betterment and eventual independence of backward people and proclaimed their own "genius for colonisation". Some empire-builders were, indeed, sceptical about the possibilities of progress, especially in the short run. As one Viceroy of India said: "We are trying to do in half a century what in other countries has occupied the life of a Nation." And indeed most of his kind promoted, as one of them wrote: "Sanitation, Education, Hospitals, Roads, Bridges, Navigation".

No one toiled more assiduously than Lord Curzon, Viceroy from 1899 to 1905, who (as *The Times* remarked) took to government as other men took to drink. Managing to combine pomp and pomposity with wit and ability, this grandest of Grand Ornamentals introduced large measures of justice, reform and public welfare. He also had a passion for detail, so much so that he even ordered the removal of pigeon droppings from Calcutta's Public Library. Curzon virtually reconstructed the raj, which he hoped would last for a thousand years.

His boldest initiative was to partition the province of Bengal, splitting the Hindu west from the Muslim east in a flagrant attempt to divide and rule. This Roman policy had some success. It prompted the formation of a Muslim League which claimed to represent a nation within the nation. But it also galvanised the largely Hindu Indian National Congress, founded in 1885, to campaign more vigorously for independence. Moreover Curzon stirred up a spirit of militant patriotism not seen since the Mutiny. It was manifested in huge demonstrations, the boycott of British goods and occasional acts of terror.

This provoked a twin response, repression and concession: a crackdown by police and troops; and the provision of token Indian representation in government. In 1911, too, the British staged a magnificent durbar outside Delhi to celebrate the coronation of the King-Emperor George V. It was the culmination of a series of brilliant pageants mounted to enhance the prestige of the white rulers and to dazzle the imagination of the native masses. Oriental minds were thought to be peculiarly susceptible to the parade of power, though sophisticated Indians dismissed these spectacles as "government by entertainment".

Officials responsible for administering the Empire on the ground also put on a show to impress their charges. District Commissioners, as Somerset Maugham noted, dressed for dinner in the jungle "to maintain the proper pride" that a white man should have in himself. George Orwell explained in a well-known essay that he had shot an elephant, which had been on the rampage but no longer posed a danger, in order to sustain the dignity of his race: "A sahib has got to act like a sahib."

The Viceroy of India, George
Curzon, with his wife Mary
on the elephant "Lakshman
Prasad" in Delhi, 29
December 1902

In *A Passage to India* E. M. Forster revealed how that ubiquitous institution, the colonial club, maintained the social solidarity and racial exclusiveness of the ruling caste. The arrival of Victorian memsahibs, who superseded native concubines ("sleeping dictionaries"), contributed to the establishment of sola-topeed empire-builders as a superior order of beings. So did manly sports, such as polo, pig-sticking and tiger-shooting. So, indeed, did hard, honest, courageous, self-sacrificing labour in a bewildering variety of spheres – tax collection, legal adjudication, police supervision as well as health, welfare, education, agriculture and public works of all sorts. The dedicated service of patriarchal officials helped to make the British Empire, relatively speaking, a model of benevolence.

The so-called "little tin gods" owed their first loyalty to the Empire, however, not to the colonised masses. From the top downwards the British governed in their own interest, paying lip service to liberty but frequently flouting egalitarian ideals. "If our ancestors had cared for the rights of other people," said Lord Salisbury, "the British Empire would not have been made." Its purpose was to strengthen the mother country with transfusions of alien vitality, though, Salisbury warned, "as India must be bled, the bleeding should be done judiciously". Thus British rule was arbitrary, irresponsible and often just plain bad. During the famines which caused 30 million deaths in India between 1860 and 1908, the authorities did not strive officiously to keep the victims alive and, as Curzon acknowledged, such disasters excited no more interest at home than a squall on the Serpentine.

Similarly, by sanctioning the export of several million indentured labour-ers between 1820 and 1920, to work on plantations from Fiji to Trinidad, the Indian government presided over a new form of bondage. At a local level there were innumerable examples of despotism on the part of petty officials, many of them boorish, racist and reactionary products of English public schools. Risk-ing disease, madness and death in the heart of darkness, they often succumbed to drink, sloth or lust – the Empire was always a field for sexual adventure. Insolent aloofness was almost universal and kicking coolies was standard prac-tice. There were also instances of corruption – it was said that PWD, the initials of India's Public Works Department, really stood for Plunder Without Danger. George Orwell, who witnessed colonial dirty work at close quarters as a policeman in Burma, apparently burned with hatred for his own country-men and longed for a native revolt that would "drown their Empire in blood".

Despite huge imperial enterprises such as the construction of railways, the British often barely scratched the surface of their subjects' lives. By 1947 40,000 miles of track had been laid in India, primarily as a means of

King George V and Queen Mary at the Delhi Durbhar, 1911

defence (like Roman roads) as well as a source of profit. Yet the permanent way did little to relieve famines – it actually permitted dealers to transport grain from stricken areas to hoarding centres. In richer colonies the British were able to foster progress, for example by creating the Malayan tin smelting industry. They could even afford extravagances. In Kuala Lumpur they erected a spectacular white and gold railway station embellished with minarets, spires, cupolas, scalloped eaves and keyhole arches, an architectural style described as "Late Marzipan".

But in poorer possessions, tropical slums such as the West Indies and the Pacific islands, remote wilds such as the southern Sudan and north Borneo, the empire-builders pursued a policy of salutary neglect, dealing with the inhabitants on "a care and maintenance basis". India itself was hardly better served. In the last days of the raj a new Governor of (reunited) Bengal complained that his starving province had,

> practically speaking, no irrigation or drainage, a medieval system of agriculture, no roads, no education, no cottage industries, completely inadequate hospitals, no effective public health services… There are not even plans to make good these deficiencies.

Even during its noon-time grandeur the British Empire had little claim to glory.

THE BRITISH JOHN BULL AND THE AMERICAN UNCLE SAM BEAR THE WHITE MAN'S BURDEN. JUDGE MAGAZINE, APRIL, 1899

"THE WHITE

ge

IGNORANCE

OPPRESSION

BARBARISM

CUBA

N'S BURDEN."

Chapter Ten

AFTERMATH OF ARMAGEDDON

The British Empire made a crucial contribution to the Allied victory in the First World War. Nearly a third of the troops who served King and Country abroad came from India and the four "white" dominions. They fought not only in Europe but in the Middle East, where 700,000 sepoys destroyed the Turkish hegemony, and in Africa, where the German colonies fell to largely South African forces. Equally vital was the colonial provision of money, munitions and raw materials.

The sacrificial solidarity of Greater Britain, which increasingly adopted the name Commonwealth, was all the more impressive since the war occasioned the collapse of the Russian, German, Austro-Hungarian and Ottoman empires. And the peace treaties added some two million square miles to the British Empire, in the shape of territories mandated under the League of Nations such as Palestine, Mesopotamia, Transjordan and Tanganyika. Lord Curzon, now Foreign Secretary, had some reason to proclaim that

The British flag has never flown over a more powerful and united empire... Never did our voice count for more in the councils of nations; or in determining the future destinies of mankind.

Indian Cavalry on the Western front in 1914

King George V expressed it less majestically: "we are the Top Dog".

Yet the Great War inflicted great damage on the British Empire. Most obviously, it exacted a frightful toll in blood and treasure. About 725,000 Britons were killed, many of them young officers, a lost generation of empire-builders. The war cost £9 billion, increasing the National Debt by a factor of fourteen and constraining future expenditure on the Empire. Military disasters such as Gallipoli and Passchendaele impaired British prestige. Indians hoped and expected that national freedom would be their reward for defending the Empire. Inspired by T. E. Lawrence to revolt against the Turks, Arabs were incensed when the Allies broke their (anyway inconsistent) war-time promises, notably by replacing Muslim with Christian rule over much of the Middle East and by establishing a Jewish homeland in Palestine.

The conflict caused widespread disruption in Africa where it marked, as Harry Johnston said, "the beginning of revolt against the white man's supremacy". The Easter Rising and the Bolshevik Revolution stimulated independence movements throughout the Empire. It was further destabilised by President Woodrow Wilson's declarations about the "equality of nations" and the need for "self-determination". Even the territorial gains afforded by the mandates seemed something of a liability. The Empire's very size, it was

Emir Feisal's delegation at Versailles, during the Paris Peace Conference of 1919.
Feisal is at the front. T. E. Lawrence is on his left, just behind him.

thought, sapped its strength. Like Rome, to which it was often compared, it was endangered by what Gibbon had called "immoderate greatness". The socialist Beatrice Webb reckoned that the British Empire was suffering from "a sort of senile hypertrophy". It was likened to a gorged giant, gouty at the extremities.

Egypt, guarding the Empire's lifeline, was an especially tender spot. When Turkey sided with Germany in 1914, the British had repudiated Ottoman overlordship and formally made Egypt a protectorate, replacing Khedive Abbas with Sultan (later King) Fuad. Martial law was imposed along with heavy war-time burdens, among them higher taxes and the direction of labour. In 1919 discontent flared into violence when the foremost nationalist politician, Said Zaghlul, was arrested for agitating to put the case for Egyptian autonomy to the peace conference in Paris. Riots, strikes and killings multiplied as *effendi* and *fellaheen* united in opposition to the occupying power. The British retaliated fiercely, bombing and machine-gunning crowds.

Lloyd George feared that Zaghlul might "create a Pan-Islamic Sinn Féin machine" which would cause mischief in other parts of the Empire. So the

Welsh Wizard reluctantly adopted Milner's scheme to make Egypt *"appear more independent"* while retaining the substance of imperial power. In 1922, after a long wrangle during which the uncompromising Zaghlul was exiled, Britain recognised Egypt as an independent sovereign state. But the Union Jack continued to fly over the High Commissioner's Residency in Cairo, which remained the source of military, financial and much administrative control. King Fuad grumbled in 1935 that his prime minister "dared not move a pencil on his desk without Residency advice".

In that year, however, Mussolini's invasion of Ethiopia disclosed the fundamental weakness of Britain's overstretched Empire. Beset by the Depression and alarmed by the dictators, Stanley Baldwin's government was too feeble even to deny Italian ships passage through the Suez Canal. As a result Egypt became exposed to Fascist aggression from Ethiopia as well as from Libya. So in 1936 an Anglo-Egyptian treaty was negotiated, stipulating that Egypt should join the League of Nations and that Britain should garrison the Canal Zone only, while ceasing to monopolise control of the Sudanese condominium. Yet although the British High Commissioner in Cairo became a mere ambassador, he continued to pull the strings and the sybaritic new king, Farouk, danced to his tune – when he wasn't dancing in night clubs or ogling his favourite belly dancer, Tahia Carioca, known to the British as Gippy Tummy.

In Khartoum, though, where no consultation about the Sudan's fate had taken place, the treaty caused outrage. Post-war nationalist agitation had culminated in a military insurrection in 1924, quickly crushed. Thereafter the colonial power had attempted to quarantine the country against democratic infection. It fostered limited development in the Arab Muslim north and sanctioned total stagnation in the African pagan south, suppressing endemic unrest by means of near-genocidal expeditions that involved aerial bombardments and what one district officer called "regular Congo atrocities". But in 1938, as opposition to the treaty hardened, the Sudan's educated elite formed a Graduates' General Congress, on the Indian model. It skilfully exploited the differences between London and Cairo. And it presaged the demise of another elite, the Sudan Political Service, which was so full of Oxbridge sportsmen that their vast Nile domain had been described as "a Land of Blacks ruled by Blues".

Mesopotamia – that artificial combination of three diverse Ottoman provinces, Mosul, Baghdad and Basra, which is modern Iraq – also rebelled against being incorporated into an infidel empire. In 1920 tribal forces declared *jihad*, ravaged the countryside and threatened the capital. The British responded fiercely on the ground and also employed air power, a revolutionary means of imperial control, to devastating effect. The War

Secretary, Winston Churchill, who remarked that Arabs lived largely on camel dung, also favoured "using poisonous gas against uncivilised tribes". But when the revolt had been quelled, at a cost of nearly 10,000 lives, Churchill, now Colonial Secretary, sought a cut-price compromise. He secured the enthronement of the Emir Feisal, who had fought with Lawrence in Arabia, as King of Iraq, his elevation being confirmed by a rigged plebiscite.

In 1922 the royal puppet was obliged to sign a treaty of alliance which confirmed Britain's paramount position in his new realm. Although this position was disguised by the appointment of many Iraqi officials, agitation for truly national sovereignty continued. Fearing Bolshevik infiltration as well as interference from a renascent Turkey, and keen to exploit Iraq's newly discovered oil resources, the British resisted. But in 1930 Ramsay Macdonald's Labour government agreed to a new treaty granting Iraq a large degree of independence while retaining control over defence and other matters. Two years later the mandate ceased and Iraq joined the League of Nations. The Anglo-Iraqi relationship remained volatile, as evidenced by the pro-Axis coup in 1941. But until 1958, when the monarchy was overthrown, Britain retained substantial influence in a country so divided that it was almost impossible to rule save by unbridled oppression.

Palestine was a thorn in the side of the Empire between the world wars, partly because it was a "twice-promised land". In 1916 the British had offered it to the Arabs in return for rebelling against the Turks. But the following year, when the war was going badly, perfidious Albion sought the support of "international Jewry" (itself an anti-Semitic concept) by issuing the Balfour Declaration. This promised "a national home for the Jewish people" in Palestine while pledging that nothing would be done to prejudice the rights of non-Jews. Opponents of the Declaration pointed out its inconsistency and its injustice. Arabs constituted ninety per cent of the population and their title to the land rested on long occupation and deep attachment rather than on the Old Testament – on historical grounds, said Curzon, the British had a better claim to parts of France than the Jews had to Palestine. Critics also warned that a Jewish homeland would become a Zionist state. This was doubtless what Lloyd George and Balfour had in mind: to establish a colonial dominion by proxy, a Jewish outpost of the Empire which would pen the French into a diminished Syria, counter-balance an Arab Transjordan and guard the Suez Canal.

Instead the Holy Land became an arena of unholy strife. Arabs protested against even a modest new influx of Jews, which had the irritating effect, said Palestine's first High Commissioner, of "an alien body in living flesh".

Disturbances were commonplace, spiking in 1919 and 1929. The British tried to stem immigration and to mediate between what one official called "a tiresome gaggle of yids and wogs". In 1936 Arab strikes, boycotts, riots, bombings and assassinations multiplied, prompted by the arrival of 166,000 Jews in three years, most of them fleeing Nazi persecution. The skirmishes became a full-scale uprising in 1938-9, all the more vicious for involving Jews as well as Britons. Having contemplated partition, Neville Chamberlain's government extended its appeasement policy to the Levant, imposing strict limits on immigration and land purchase, and promising an independent Arab-dominated Palestine. This in turn provoked a Jewish campaign of violence and terror, which cost several thousand lives and was only interrupted by World War Two. Far from building an imperial New Jerusalem, the British found in Palestine what a senior administrator would call, quoting the historian Josephus, "a golden bowl full of scorpions".

Conflict erupted elsewhere in the Empire. Another Afghan war broke out in 1919, ending the remnants of British control in Kabul. In 1920 British forces in Somaliland finally defeated the Dervish leader, Mohammed Hassan, nicknamed by his enemies the "Mad Mullah". Nationalist organisations sprang up in Burma and Malaya. Hong Kong was shaken by serious labour troubles. New strong men, Mustapha Kemal in Turkey and Reza Khan in Persia, further undermined Britain's position in the Middle East. Nowhere, though, was the situation more menacing than in the barbican of the Empire, India. Here the war had given a massive boost to the independence movement. It had also demonstrated how integral the subcontinent was to Britain's greatness. In the words of Lord Curzon: "As long as we rule India, we are the greatest power in the world. If we lose it we shall drop straight away to a third rate power." The scene was set for a momentous struggle.

T. E. LAWRENCE, 1888-1935

T.E. Lawrence in 1919

Lawrence of Arabia was the British Empire's last action hero. At a time when the glory of war was dissolving in the mud of Flanders, he inspired a desert revolt against Ottoman rule which helped to give Britain a heady new (though short-lived) role in the Middle East. And he himself became famous when an American journalist, Lowell Thomas, created a romantic extravaganza out of the Arab uprising, with Lawrence as its star. Lawrence burnished his own legend in The Seven Pillars of Wisdom (1926), a massive, complex, richly dramatic but often fantastic autobiographical account.

Critics said that everything in it was true except the facts and Lawrence confessed to being a man of masks and a bag of tricks. He portrayed himself as an imperfect Arabian knight, plagued by pride, remorse, doubt and humiliation.

Lawrence early learned to conceal his identity, being the illegitimate son of a minor Anglo-Irish nobleman and a puritanical Scottish governess. She beat him as a boy, perhaps stimulating his lifelong, sado-masochistic fascination with pain. Lawrence was brought up in Oxford, distinguished himself at the University and became an archaeologist, specialising in Syrian Crusader castles. In 1914 he joined the Arab Bureau in Cairo as an intelligence officer of rare intelligence. Two years later he liaised with Feisal, son of the Emir of Mecca, who was willing to back the Allies in return for Arab independence.

Bedouin forces concentrated on attacking Turkish communications and Lawrence himself took part in many raids. He also

Camel–mounted Arab troops on the march in the desert near Jebel Serd, March 1917

rode in the triumphant charge on the port of Aqaba in 1917, accidentally shooting his own camel in the head. The desert campaign culminated in the capture of Damascus in 1918, when tribal irregulars afforded fierce assistance to General Allenby's army. But this victory did not win Arab freedom. The Allies had made contradictory promises about the future of the Middle East, and the post-war Palestinian, Jordanian, Mesopotamian, Syrian and Lebanese mandates amounted to imperial expansion by other means. Lawrence himself favoured a federation of semi-autonomous Arab states under British tutelage. He also supported the RAF's bombing of Iraqi insurgents and Jewish immigration to Palestine. All told, he was implicated in betraying the Arab cause.

Ambiguity was the essential dimension of Lawrence's existence. He craved fame but shunned publicity. After the war he tried to hide in the armed services as Private Shaw and Aircraftman Ross. Perhaps his conspicuous anonymity was intended to conceal a homosexual bent common to other empire-builders, among them Gordon, Rhodes, Kitchener and Baden-Powell. The enigma was compounded by the official secrecy shrouding the motor-bicycle accident that killed Lawrence at the age of forty-six. Part-genius, part-charlatan, he continues to intrigue posterity. With the possible exception of General Gordon, he remains the most charismatic of all imperial adventurers.

Chapter Eleven

THE PASSING OF THE RAJ

Abright new chapter in India's history seemed about to open immediately after the Great War. Britain made various overtures to its people, the most important of which was to introduce, as a first step towards self-rule, a system of power-sharing known as dyarchy. This devolved control over matters such as health, education and agriculture to Indian provincial authorities while leaving a somewhat more representative central government in charge of taxation, defence and foreign policy. However, Indians were bitterly disappointed by such a meagre return for their war-time sacrifice and there was a storm of protest.

The British responded by passing the Rowlatt Act, subjecting those accused of sedition to arbitrary arrest and detention. This prompted further agitation, often violent, especially in the Punjab. Stern repressive measures were imposed, which led to one of the worst atrocities in imperial history. On 13 April 1919 General Reginald Dyer ordered his troops to open fire on an illegal but peaceful gathering in a walled space known as the Jallianwala Bagh near the Golden Temple of Amritsar. At least 379 people were killed, many of them children, and the wounded numbered some 1,500. Dyer was widely condemned, even by Winston Churchill, but many of his compatriots praised him for having averted another Mutiny. Dyer himself publicly asserted that he had

GANDHI AND NEHRU
IN 1942

Gandhi with the Viceroy, Lord Mountbatten, 1947

done "a jolly lot of good". Privately he boasted that the massacre "would teach the bloody browns a lesson". The refined young nationalist Jawaharlal Nehru happened to hear this remark when he encountered Dyer on an overnight train journey to Delhi, during which he was also offended by the General's shocking-pink striped pyjamas.

Nehru concluded that Dyer's "demoniac deeds", as Congress called them, exemplified the "brutal and immoral" nature of imperialism. Rather than advocating retaliation in kind, however, the radical Nehru succumbed to the influence of the new champion of "soul force" or passive resistance, Mohandas Gandhi, dubbed Mahatma – great soul. A westernised human rights lawyer transformed into a Hindu sage, Gandhi now became the guru of the Congress Party and the most charismatic foe of the raj. Declaring that it was sinful to cooperate with a "satanic" government, he led a campaign of civil disobedience against it. In 1921 he even organised a boycott of the Prince of Wales's Indian tour. Churchill thought that Gandhi "ought to be laid, bound hand and foot, at the gates of Delhi and then trampled on by an enormous elephant with the new Viceroy seated on its back".

Unable to galvanise national resistance to the raj and concerned that his campaign was causing violence, Gandhi called it off in 1922, much to Nehru's

Jinnah with Gandhi in Bombay, 1944

fury. Yet the secular firebrand and the otherworldly ascetic together opposed the all-white Commission led by Sir John Simon in 1928 to consider reforming the dyarchy system. The liberal Tory Viceroy Lord Irwin (later Lord Halifax) took the sting out of their protest by affirming that India was on the road to dominion status. To regain the initiative Gandhi hit on the inspired tactic of leading a march to the sea in order to gather salt without paying tax on what was a gift of God. Millions followed suit and Nehru said that Gandhi had created a new India by his "magic touch". But the demonstrations turned violent, all the more so when the Mahatma was arrested in May 1930. The government outlawed Congress and locked up over 60,000 of its supporters. To resolve the impasse, Irwin freed the half-naked fakir (Churchill's term) and negotiated a relaxation of repression in return for a halt to non-cooperation. The Viceroy, who entertained the teetotal Gandhi in his splendid new Lutyens-designed Government House, was accused of taking tea with treason.

Irwin's successor, Lord Willingdon, reversed his policy. He cracked down hard and effectively on Congress, confessing that he was "becoming a sort of Mussolini of India". At the same time, the British pushed through a Government of India Bill (1935), which gave the provinces virtual self-rule and extended the principle of dyarchy to the central government. Churchill warned that the Bill would sound the death "knell of the British Empire in the East". But its purpose was to perpetuate the raj and Nehru denounced it as a charter of slavery. Following Gandhi's advice, however, the Congress Party went to the polls and won power in most provinces, though the scheme of national federation foundered on the opposition of the princes, avid to protect their privileges. More ominously, the very success of Congress, which was dominated by Hindus, provoked the cry "Islam in danger". Mohammad Ali Jinnah, the gaunt, implacable, chain-smoking and whisky-drinking leader of the Muslim League, told the Viceroy that if Britain were planning to abandon the subcontinent his co-religionists must "bestir themselves and be ready to fight".

An overseas fight supervened in September 1939 when the Viceroy, now Lord Linlithgow, declared that India was at war with Germany. Gandhi sympathised with the anti-Nazi cause, describing Jews as the Untouchables of Christianity. But Linlithgow refused to give a clear promise of self-rule in return for nationalist support and Nehru said that Indians must not shed their blood to keep their chains. Thus Congress members resigned from their offices, leaving local authority in British hands, and many engaged in further acts of civil disobedience. Over 25,000 arrests followed, including that of Nehru himself, who was treated like a common criminal. When Churchill became Prime Minister he took an even tougher line. He also exploited the

General Reginald Dyer

growing "Hindu-Moslem feud", which he regarded as "a bulwark of British rule in India". Nor was Churchill deflected by the Atlantic Charter, agreed with President Franklin Roosevelt in 1941, which stated that all peoples had the right to choose their own government. The Prime Minister blithely announced that the Charter did not apply to the British Empire – which Roosevelt considered a "world tyranny".

When Japan entered the war, ripping through the flimsy fabric of Britain's eastern Empire and threatening India, Churchill was reluctantly persuaded to rally support there by offering independence after the Allied victory. A mission led by Sir Stafford Cripps, a vegetarian, teetotal socialist known to the Prime Minister as Sir Stifford Crapps, arrived in Delhi to thrash out the details. But Churchill undermined him, Gandhi refused to accept "a post-dated cheque" and Congress rejected proposals that did not guarantee a free and united India. Instead the party mounted another civil disobedience campaign, its slogan being "Quit India". This led to major disturbances throughout the subcontinent which left thousands dead. Linlithgow acted fiercely and effectively to quell what he regarded as the most serious revolt since the Mutiny. Gandhi, Nehru and other leaders were imprisoned along with tens of thousands of the rank and file. Defying liberal opposition to colonialism and appealing for Allied unity, Churchill famously declared that he would not "preside over the liquidation of the British Empire".

He was unmoved by Gandhi's hunger strikes and callous about the famine that had killed some three million Bengalis by 1944. He refused to send scarce relief ships to Calcutta, saying that anyway Indians would go on breeding "like rabbits". Leo Amery accused him of having a "Hitler-like attitude" towards India. Keen to refute such charges as the 1945 election approached, Churchill entered into negotiations with Congress and the Muslim League. He correctly anticipated that they would be wrecked by communal antagonism, since Jinnah proposed that the only way of preventing Hindu dictatorship was to create a separate Islamic state – Pakistan.

So Clement Attlee's new Labour government had to resolve the Indian conundrum. Opposed to imperialism, his party was, as its deputy leader Herbert Morrison said, "great friends with the jolly old empire". But although ministers wanted to preserve Britain's global position, they were committed to Indian independence. Indeed, what with near-bankruptcy, post-war demobilisation and further Indian unrest, including several mutinies, they were in no position to stop it.

In 1946 another British mission, again involving Cripps, failed to secure agreement about the shape of a self-governing India: Jinnah wanted a federal structure to protect Muslims but Nehru insisted on a strong central authority. Meanwhile the subcontinent was riven by communal violence. As imperial control slipped away, plans were made to evacuate the personnel of the raj, code-named Operation Bedlam and Operation Madhouse. Attlee deplored anything that looked like Operation Scuttle, an Asian Dunkirk.

To secure an orderly withdrawal he appointed Admiral Lord Mountbatten as last Viceroy. Handsome, vainglorious and royal, Mountbatten soon concluded that partition was unavoidable. Gandhi decried "the vivisection of the motherland". But she was already tearing herself apart as Hindus, Muslims and Sikhs continued to murder each other, and Mountbatten believed that only iron surgery could avert full-scale civil war. So he announced that India and Pakistan would become separate, independent states on 15 August 1947. The raj, which had taken 200 years to construct, would be liquidated in seventy-three days.

Mountbatten bullied and cajoled nearly all the princes into accepting the settlement. He also persuaded a reluctant Nehru and a willing Jinnah to stay in the Commonwealth. But he favoured the former and evidently influenced the boundary commission to the disadvantage of Pakistan. Moreover Mountbatten acted so precipitately (and was so preoccupied with starring in the gorgeous handover ceremonies) that he failed to take proper precautions against the carnage and chaos caused by territorial dismemberment. As it was slaughter and rapine took place on an inconceivable scale. Atrocities abounded and the Punjab ran with "rivers of blood". All told, a million people were killed and eleven million displaced. Such was the tragic culmination of British rule.

Yet, as Nehru proclaimed, India awoke to "life and freedom". And Britain congratulated itself on the emancipation of a fifth of the human race. Indeed the transfer of power was represented as a deliberate fulfilment of a longstanding trust: a subject people had been brought to maturity under the imperial wing and was now entitled its birthright – nationhood. To be sure, apologists for the Empire had often claimed that its goal was colonial self-government. But this had always seemed a distant prospect and it was necessary to justify the abrupt withdrawal from the subcontinent. So the myth was promulgated that Indian independence had been won, not forced. Ceding it was mark of Commonwealth strength not imperial, still less national, weakness. The raj had vanished and King George VI was sad that he could no longer sign himself RI (Rex et Imperator) but Britain had acquired two new Dominions under the crown. Despite the loss of India few thought that the stupendous structure of the British Empire faced imminent collapse.

Chapter Twelve

ORIENTAL REGRESS

If the extinction of the Indian raj did not seem to presage the end of the colonial era, there was no denying that the British Empire in the orient had suffered ruinous damage during the Second World War. It had long been surviving on prestige, the shadow of power, and this was fatally impaired by the forces of Nippon. Churchill and his ilk had derided the Japanese as the "wops of Asia" and "coolies in uniform". But Emperor Hirohito's forces advanced more swiftly than those of Genghis Khan. They took Hong Kong in seventeen days. On 10 December 1941 their aircraft sank two of the Royal Navy's mightiest warships, *Prince of Wales* and *Repulse*. The soldiers of the sun, many riding bicycles, raced through the supposedly impenetrable jungles of Malaya, brushing aside imperial troops. Then they seized Singapore before driving the British out of Burma and menacing Ceylon. Churchill described the capture of the "Gibraltar of the East" and its 130,000-strong garrison as "the worst disaster and the greatest capitulation in British history". Subhas Chandra Bose, extreme nationalist leader of the Indian National Army allied to the Japanese, said that Singapore was "the graveyard of the British Empire".

In Burma, one official wrote, the Japanese "destroyed the myth of western invincibility". They also exploded the illusion of white supremacy. Throughout the country, as George Orwell had earlier observed, "anti-European feeling was very bitter". And at the triumphant (though devastating) advance of an Asiatic race, said Ba Maw, "Burmese hearts beat wildly". Aung San's Burmese National Army donned Japanese uniforms and opposed the British, only to change sides once it was apparent that the Allies were winning.

Aung San himself emerged as the outstanding nationalist leader in 1945 and immediately made it clear that half-hearted British attempts to restore imperial rule would not be tolerated. "We Burmese are not the Burmese of 1942," he declared, "and if we have to use force and fight we are fully prepared." Stirring up nationwide agitation, he made the country virtually ungovernable. Indeed, he obliged Attlee to recall the vacillating Governor, Sir Reginald Dorman-Smith, who punned: "I depart 'Unhonoured and Aung San'."

Chronically short of manpower, Dorman-Smith's successor, General Hubert Rance, was unable to stem the chaos, which was compounded by rural banditry, Communist insurgency, ethnic rivalry and acute labour unrest. So he virtually ceded power to Aung San, who came to London (looking unprecedentedly smart in a uniform that Nehru had had specially tailored for him) to settle terms on which his country would become a sovereign state. Attlee feared that an armed rebellion was imminent in Burma. So he sacrificed the interests of Britain's minority clients such as the Karens, Kachens and Shan, in order to achieve the swift birth of a nation that would, he hoped, remain inside the Commonwealth.

The hope was dashed after the assassination of Aung San by political opponents, a sinister augury of the country's brutal future. But astrologers chose a propitious moment for Burma to become independent: 4.20 am on 4 January 1948. There were joyous celebrations. Popular dramatic performances represented "a free people dancing in a rain of gold and silver".

Exactly a month later Ceylon gained its independence, thanks in part to Aung San. He had forced the British to relinquish Burma despite its wartime support for Japan and they could therefore hardly hold on to Ceylon, which had remained loyal to the Allies. Moreover, where Aung San mouthed menaces, D. S. Senanayake made his demands in a spirit of good will and cooperation. Lord Soulbury, whose 1945 report recommended that Ceylon should have full self-government apart from defence and foreign affairs, said the Sinhalese leader resembled "the best type of English country-gentleman".

Senanayake accepted Soulbury's conditions as a means to an end. But he insisted, in suitably bucolic terms, that Ceylon was still a tethered cow and must be let loose completely. The Labour Colonial Secretary, Arthur Creech Jones, agreed but worried that he would be accused of "squandering the Empire". He therefore argued that Ceylon, politically stable and strategically

Aung San and family in 1947

vital, was a special case long groomed for self-rule, and that as a non-white dominion it would actually help to preserve the Empire. By remaining under the crown it would demonstrate that the Commonwealth was no "mere afterglow following sunset, ending in night".

For almost a decade Britain made no further grants of independence east of Suez and during this time it fought to hang on to Malaya. The best advertisement for its rule was the tyrannical occupation of the Japanese, which had involved much bloodshed and a merciless exploitation of the country's resources. Resistance to Nippon had come largely from the Chinese half of the population and when their guerrillas emerged from the jungle in 1945 they inflicted a reign of terror on real and supposed collaborators, mostly Malay, who retaliated with equal ferocity.

To suppress the anarchy the British initially used Japanese troops, thus delaying their repatriation, a vast operation code-named "Nipoff". Once in control the imperial authorities proposed to establish progressive rule, reflecting socialist ideals. But the Labour government's prime need, at a time of acute economic crisis, was to extract profit from the Empire. Tin and rubber were huge earners of hard currency and Malaya became Britain's "dollar arsenal". Its people called the British *lintah puteh*, white leeches.

End of empire? The surrender of Allied forces in Singapore, 15 February 1942

In 1948, amid continuing turmoil, a Malayan Federation was set up which went some way to meeting the demands of Dato Onn, flamboyant leader of the newly formed United Malays National Organisation (UMNO). But many Chinese felt threatened and a young Maoist commander, Chin Peng, breathed fresh life into the Communist insurgency, murderously attacking plantations and mines. A state of emergency was declared and the security forces took increasingly harsh measures against the "bandits" – in December 1948 the Scots Guards massacred at least twenty-three Chinese at Batang Kali in Selangor.

In 1950 the army began moving hundreds of thousands of Chinese into fortified villages so as to deny aid to the "Communist terrorists", as they were now termed. This programme, comparable to the establishment of concentration camps during the Boer War, was continued by General Sir Gerald Templer, sent out as High Commissioner in 1952 to succeed Sir Henry Gurney who had been killed in an ambush. Templer was ruthless, employing chemical defoliants and defending the decapitation of guerrillas. But he also made sterling efforts to win Malayan "hearts and minds". He shocked Europeans by shaking hands with his servants.

In what was one of Britain's last major imperial struggles, Templer owed his success to the enemy's weakness. Many Chinese were pro-British and anti-Communist and Chin Peng was forced to retreat into Thailand. But as the French defeat at Dien Bien Phu in Vietnam demonstrated, time was running out for western powers in the east by 1954. Even ministers in Churchill's cabinet no longer believed that Britain could continue in the traditional fashion to hold dominion over palm and pine. But they hoped that British influence in Asia could be sustained if a pacified, self-governing Malaya joined the Commonwealth. This outcome became more likely when a shrewd playboy prince, Tunku Abdul Rahman, who succeeded Dato Onn as Leader of UMNO, allied with Chinese and Indian political organisations to win at the polls in 1955. His majority in the Federal Legislative Council proved irresistible and two years later Malaya achieved *Merdeka* – independence.

Singapore, then a crown colony in its own right, also shook off British rule. But its first prime minister, Lee Kuan Yew, elected in 1959, did not envisage that it would become a separate city state. In fact, Singapore joined the confederation of Malaysia, which included Sarawak and north Borneo (Sabah), in 1963. Harold Macmillan's government supported this merger, which parcelled up former colonies into an anti-Communist bloc, thus enhancing the Commonwealth. However British forces became heavily embroiled in Malaysia's "Confrontation" with an aggressive Indonesia. This wound down in 1965, the year in which the Tunku expelled Chinese-dominated Singapore from the Malayasian federation, but Lee Kuan Yew still looked for protection to the former imperial power.

He was therefore appalled when Britain, assailed by one economic trouble after another, decided to evacuate its great base in 1967, pulling out of South East Asia and keeping only a token military presence in Singapore (until 1976). Yet as a schoolboy at Raffles College in February 1942, Lee had detected the shape of things to come. When the British, vainly trying to halt the Japanese advance on Lion City, blew up the causeway linking the island to the mainland, the headmaster had asked what the explosion was. Lee replied: "That is the end of the British Empire."

Chapter Thirteen

MIDDLE EAST MISFORTUNES

Despite quitting India, Attlee's government attached supreme importance to maintaining Britain's position in the Suez region. The Canal provided the shortest sea route to its oriental and East African colonies. It was also a vital channel for Arab oil supplies at a time when the Cold War was emerging from the ashes of the hot one. Anthony Eden had said that the defence of the eastern Mediterranean was a matter of life and death to the Empire and his successor at the Foreign Office, the formidable trade unionist Ernest Bevin, believed that keeping the Levant in the British sphere of influence was crucial to "our position as a great power". In fact Labour's imperial stance was only marginally less bullish than that of the Tories and Bevin was said to have dropped nothing from Eden's foreign policy but the aitches.

The most acute problem Bevin faced in 1945 was what to do about Palestine, still a mandated territory but now held under the auspices of the United Nations. Most Jews and Arabs had supported the Allies against the Axis during the war, though zealots from both communities saw the British as their more immediate foes. Abraham Stern, for example, wished to "shout 'Heil Hitler' in Jerusalem" and his Gang carried out terrorist acts against the occupying power, notably the assassination in 1944 of Churchill's friend Lord Moyne, Resident Minister in the Middle East. Churchill had already modi-

Egyptian President Gamal Abdel Nasser waving to crowds in Mansoura from a train car

fied his pro-Jewish position to avoid alienating the Arabs and he now equated Zionism with gangsterism, shunning the Jewish leader Chaim Weizmann. But as the truth about the Holocaust emerged, many Gentiles (especially in America) concluded that only a Jewish state could avert another such catastrophe. Arabs protested that they should not have to pay the debt Europeans owed to the Jews for their sufferings and that Muslims would become the innocent victims of a unique brand of Judeo-Christian imperialism. Bevin reluctantly heeded their case. He restricted Jewish immigration to Palestine, appearing indifferent to the plight of those described by David Ben-Gurion, Israel's first prime minister, as "refugees from hell".

Zionists in the Holy Land mounted a bitter offensive against the British authorities. They smuggled in immigrants, evading a naval blockade and defying an increasingly repressive state. They promoted strikes, initiated riots and launched attacks against British troops and installations. Fierce retaliation was followed by savage reprisal, notably the bombing of Jerusalem's King David Hotel in 1946, which killed 91 people. When the British hanged Jewish terrorists, Menachem Begin's Irgun organisation responded by hanging two army sergeants and booby-trapping their bodies – an event which resulted in swastikas being daubed on synagogues in England. The British had no stomach for this quasi-colonial struggle: it opened them to charges of

British paratroopers at Suez, 1956

anti-Semitism; it damaged Anglo-American relations; it aggravated Arab-Jewish hostility; it engaged 100,000 men and cost £40 million a year; and it was strategically futile since, as Hugh Dalton, Chancellor of the Exchequer said, you cannot "have a secure base on top of a wasps' nest".

So Bevin referred the Palestinian question to the United Nations, which unexpectedly voted for partition. He then confirmed the British decision to surrender the mandate, which would take place on 15 May 1948. However he regarded the territorial allotment as unfair to the Arabs and the High Commissioner, Sir Alan Cunningham, had to see out his final six months without having an authority to which he could hand over power. Cunningham asked the Colonial Secretary forlornly: "Is the last soldier to see the last locomotive into the engine shed, lock the door and keep the key?" As it was British troops had the hideous task of trying to hold the ring as communal strife intensified. Terror became rampant. But the Jews were better organised and they carried out a number of massacres, notoriously at Deir Yassin, in order to drive out the Arabs. A quarter of a million were expelled or fled in what Ben-Gurion called an ethnic "clean out". As the British departed, the new state of Israel was proclaimed.

It repulsed the subsequent invasion of neighbouring Arab countries, though Transjordan, independent since 1946 under "Mr Bevin's Little King" Abdullah, did manage to capture the West Bank of the Jordan River. More important from London's viewpoint, the defeat further discredited King Farouk's regime in Egypt, where the Canal Zone (an area the size of Wales) was still occupied by British forces. They came under attack from Egyptian militants and in 1952 an army putsch ousted Farouk.

Colonel Gamal Abdel Nasser, a charismatic revolutionary, emerged as leader of the new Egyptian republic. He was determined to gain complete control of his country. Winston Churchill, once again Prime Minister, clung to his old imperial faith – as he demonstrated in 1953 by supporting a secret American coup in Iran, fraught with dire long-term consequences, which secured its oil supplies for the West. However, Churchill was persuaded that the hydrogen bomb made Suez less strategically important and that pulling out of the Canal Zone would stop Egypt from going Communist. Thus British withdrawal was scheduled for June 1956.

By this time Anthony Eden was in 10 Downing Street, eager to display the political virility of his predecessor. But he was hampered by ill health, nerve storms and overweening vanity – a model of elegance, he varnished his finger-nails and wore tailored double-breasted pyjamas. It was Nasser who proved the more potent: he was strenuously anti-imperialist, sought arms from the Soviet Union and obliged Britain to grant Sudanese independence by abandoning his country's claims to the upper Nile and thus terminating the Anglo-Egyptian condominium. Eden saw him as another Mussolini and told a Foreign Office minister, Anthony Nutting: "I want him murdered."

Instead Eden and President Eisenhower's dour Secretary of State John Foster Dulles brusquely withdrew an offer to finance the construction of the Aswan Dam. Nasser retaliated by nationalising the Suez Canal Company. Appeasement, Eden considered, would bring the British Empire to an ignoble end. Bypassing American attempts to negotiate, therefore, he entered into a conspiracy with France and Israel to overthrow Nasser by force. Some observers, like the Chief of the Air Staff, concluded that "Eden has gone bananas".

The invasion of Suez was a fiasco. It was begun by Israel and followed up by Britain and France, who pretended that they were intervening in order to separate the belligerents. The British in particular were impeded by their insistence that they were not colluding with Israel but carrying out a "police action" to "protect" the Canal (soon blocked by Nasser). Eisenhower, who had simultaneously to face voters at home and Soviet tanks in Hungary, angrily complained that his allies had double-crossed him. His refusal to prop up sterling or to help with oil supplies, along with domestic and Commonwealth opposition to the attack, quickly forced Eden to cease operations. As the last British units landed the first were being withdrawn, to make way for United

Nations peace-keepers. Eden was accused of conducting the most spectacular retreat from Suez since the time of Moses.

Harold Macmillan took over as Prime Minister in 1957, though Eisenhower feared that he was equally resistant to Britain's demise as a colonial power. Macmillan certainly posed as a patrician imperialist, but he was essentially a bourgeois pragmatist. He recognised the seismic damage that Suez had done to Britain's position – Anthony Nutting described the episode, with pardonable exaggeration, as "the dying convulsion of British imperialism". Known as the Old Entertainer, Macmillan used his theatrical and political skills to sustain an impression of British greatness. This meant mending fences with Eisenhower (whose unique version of the English language he professed to understand) and trying to give substance to the nebulous but much-vaunted "special relationship" with the United States. It meant restoring harmony in the Commonwealth, presented not as the wraith of Empire but as a butterfly emerging from the imperial chrysalis. It meant embracing change where necessary, in Africa certainly and possibly by finding a new British role inside the European community. Moreover, as Eisenhower announced his "doctrine" of stemming Communism in the Middle East, Macmillan had to show that Britain still counted in the region.

As a result he sustained bloody campaigns against liberation movements in both Cyprus and Aden. Disraeli had acquired Cyprus in 1878, extolling it as the key to Asia. In fact, the island was unimportant to, and neglected by, the British until their grip on the Middle East slackened after the Second World War. But in 1955 they resisted a guerrilla revolt aiming at union (*enosis*) with Greece, which was blessed by the wily Archbishop Makarios and led by the ruthless General Grivas. Bombings, shootings, riots and demonstrations were met with hangings, floggings and other forms of coercion, including bulldozing buildings and torturing suspects.

Furthermore, in a classic effort to divide and rule, Macmillan urged that the Turks (a fifth of the population) should be stirred up "to neutralise the Greek agitation". Thus communal violence complicated and exacerbated the anti-colonial struggle. Although Macmillan thought that a single airfield on Cyprus would serve Britain's strategic purposes, he demanded a military victory. Peace and independence came in 1960 as a result of Greco-Turkish talks but Britain retained a fig-leaf of sovereignty in the shape of two substantial military bases, enabling Macmillan to rebut any suggestion of a Middle Eastern Munich.

Aden, which had been acquired as an outpost of India in 1839, lost its imperial *raison d'être* when the raj ended in 1947. For all its fine natural harbour it was, as one diplomat said, a station on the route to nowhere. However the London government was not only conditioned by the past but fearful of a further loss of prestige after the Suez debacle. So when Nasser's Cairo Radio fomented guerrilla incursions from the desert hinterland into what it called "Occupied South Yemen", British forces became embroiled in another vicious struggle. As the uprising gathered strength in the countryside they employed tanks and aircraft, bombing villages and even poisoning crops in the hope of (as an official said) "terrorising the rebels into submission". In the port city the new National Liberation Front mounted a terror campaign of its own, aimed especially at "the running dogs of imperialism". They responded with equal savagery.

Harold Wilson, who as Labour Prime Minister often incurred charges of being unprincipled, was actually something of a romantic imperialist at heart. A keen Boy Scout in youth, he had hero-worshipped Robert Baden-Powell, the defender of Mafeking. And as late as 1965 Wilson, who presented himself as head of a global power challenging international Communism, declared that "Britain's frontiers are on the Himalayas." Yet within two years the British, capitulating to economic necessity and anticipating a complete withdrawal from the Middle East by 1971, abandoned Aden. As the last High Commissioner departed, the band of the Royal Marines played "Fings Ain't Wot They Used To Be".

Sir Anthony Eden, 1st Earl of Avon (1897-1977)

Chapter Fourteen

OUT OF AFRICA

Africa made a vast contribution in human and natural resources to the Allied cause during the Second World War, notably by providing a million fighting men. After 1945 the Labour government hoped that the continent would take the place of the Indian subcontinent as a source of national and imperial strength. Indeed, such was Britain's economic plight that it made fresh efforts to exploit its African possessions. A new cadre of officials was sent out to open up markets for British manufactured goods and to promote the supply of dollar-earning raw materials such as cotton, cocoa, coffee, palm oil and groundnuts (the Tanganyikan scheme being a notorious failure). The whole endeavour amounted to what one historian has called "a second colonial invasion". It was based on the assumption that Africans were hopelessly backward and would be incapable of ruling themselves for generations. Herbert Morrison said that granting them independence would be like giving a child of ten "a latch-key, a bank account and a shot gun".

Actually the war had had a revolutionary effect on Africa, widening horizons, developing skills, stimulating industries, encouraging the production of cash crops and bringing wage-labourers into towns where they encountered radical ideas. These were aired at a Pan-African Congress held in Manchester in 1945 which was attended by trade unionists as well as members

Queen Elizabeth II with Kwame Nkrumah during her visit to Ghana, November 1961.

of the educated elite, including future leaders such as Jomo Kenyatta and Kwame Nkrumah. The latter was a Christian Marxist and, after attending an American university, he returned home in 1947 on a mission "to throw the Europeans out of Africa."

Nkrumah found the Gold Coast, where relative affluence had created an African professional class, a good place to start. Regarding it as a "model colony", the British had already taken tentative steps towards power sharing. These did not satisfy the United Gold Coast Convention, of which Nkrumah became secretary. He widened its appeal and played on popular grievances such as unemployment among ex-servicemen. In 1948 Accra was torn by disturbances. The police fired into the rioters, who horrified Europeans by stampeding across the Oval cricket pitch during a match.

Order was restored but the Colonial Office feared that the Gold Coast might become another Burma. It therefore appointed an able new Governor, Sir Charles Arden-Clarke, charged with retaining control while bringing into office more Africans, elected under a fresh constitution. Nkrumah, who formed the militant Convention People's Party in 1949, demanded "Self-government now". He urged civil disobedience and promoted a general strike, which was accompanied by violence. Arden-Clarke imprisoned him and other leaders while the London *Daily Telegraph* portrayed his party as an alliance between Communism and "the Ju-Ju of darkest Africa". It was more like an evangelical crusade, with Nkrumah exhorting his followers to help God save the country from the imperialists. And in 1951 it won handsomely in the ballot for the Legislative Assembly. Arden-Clarke therefore released its leader and made him Prime Minister, recognising, as he put it, that Nkrumah was the only dog in his kennel.

A dog-lover himself, the Governor gave Nkrumah a bitch called Topsy as a token of friendship and the two men cooperated to achieve orderly progress towards self-government. They were hampered by serious unrest in the northern kingdom of Ashanti, where Nkrumah's increasingly messianic pretensions were detested – he took the title *Osagyefo*, Redeemer. The Colonial Secretary, Alan Lennox-Boyd, used these troubles as an excuse to postpone imperial withdrawal. But Arden-Clarke was a persuasive champion of "creative abdication", the delicate art of de-colonising at just the right pace. Eventually he convinced Lennox-Boyd, who appreciated the potency of African nationalism, that any further delay would be dangerous. In 1957, therefore, the new state of Ghana gained its independence as a member of the Commonwealth.

Nigeria followed the same trajectory. But its progress towards statehood was impeded by a baffling ethnic, linguistic, religious and cultural diversity. The largest country in tropical Africa was a colonial entity, a construct of cartography. The Nigerian version of Nkrumah, Nnamdi Azikiwe (known as Zik), who had also been educated in America and aspired to free Africans from the imperialist yoke, found it impossible to create a nationalist movement from so many atomised communities. Nevertheless he formed a political party which exploited post-war difficulties. A fiery demagogue in word and in print, he stirred up hostility to alien rule and "elec-zik-fied" his followers. However he also exacerbated regional differences, especially between the more advanced, mainly Christian Yoruba and Ibo south, and the more conservative, mainly Muslim Fulani-Hausa north. Any surrender of British power raised the prospect that, as an official put it, "our likeable, lazy northerners will be handed over to the tender mercies of the southern 'trousered apes'". One local chief feared that Nigeria would reach independence "not in peace, but in pieces."

To avert disintegration, the Colonial Office devised a new constitution in 1954. This created a federal parliament in Lagos, responsible for such matters as defence and foreign policy, but it invested regional assemblies with a large degree of autonomy. Zik rejoiced that Nigeria had been offered "self-government on a platter of gold". But it was not served up at once since further internal schisms and instances of what Nigerians called "paytriotism" seemed to promise a future of chaos and corruption. One Colonial Office mandarin warned: "the West African negro is not capable of honest democratic self-government in this generation; and probably won't be in the next."

However Nigeria could not be denied what the Gold Coast had gained, especially when, in 1958, General de Gaulle gave neighbouring French colonies the right to decide their own destiny. Rather than face increased agitation from the likes of Zik, Macmillan's government decided to bestow independence freely, speedily and amicably. So on 1 October 1960, amid hopes that another imperial liability would become a Commonwealth asset, Nigeria raised its own flag.

The year 1960 was a watershed. In February Harold Macmillan declared in Cape Town that a "wind of change" was blowing through Africa, inflating a new "national consciousness". In March Transvaal police killed 69 demonstrators at Sharpeville, focussing global opinion on the evils of *apartheid* – the issue over which South Africa would soon leave the Commonwealth. In December a momentous United Nations resolution demanded "a speedy and unconditional end to colonialism". At the same time France began to extricate itself from Algeria, and Belgium abruptly quitted the Congo. Dogged by economic problems, harried by nationalist movements and demoralised by international criticism, Britain lacked the will to sustain its Empire.

In fact Macmillan's new Colonial Secretary Iain Macleod determined to achieve decolonisation as fast as possible, especially in Africa. Here, despite his private hesitations, he became what the historian Robert Blake called "the white hope of the Blacks and the *bête noire* of the Whites". Macleod maintained convincingly that the "march of men towards their freedom can be guided, but not halted" and that acceleration was less risky than procrastination. So it was that independence arrived at a gallop in one country after another: Somalia (1960), Sierra Leone (1961), Tanganyika (1961), Uganda (1962), Kenya (1963), Zanzibar (1963), Northern Rhodesia (Zambia, 1964), Nyasaland (Malawi, 1964), Gambia (1965), Basutoland (Lesotho, 1965), Bechuanaland (Botswana, 1965), Swaziland (1968). The process of shedding these territories was relatively painless, except where there was a significant alien settler population, as in Kenya and Rhodesia.

Those who appropriated the best land in Kenya from the native inhabitants extolled it as a "white man's country". The claim was reinforced by systematic exploitation and racial discrimination, including a colour bar that excluded Africans and Asians from European amenities such as hospitals, schools, churches, hotels, cinemas and polling booths. All this was an embarrassment to the Colonial Office, which attempted to protect black- and brown-skinned people from what Churchill called "the fierce self-interest of a small white population". Its efforts were ineffective and African discontent was expressed in sporadic strikes, riots, arson attacks and cattle maimings.

In 1944 nationalists formed the Kenya African Union (KAU) with the aim of securing "land and freedom". Three years later Jomo Kenyatta became its leader. He was a Methodist-educated "mission boy" who had spent many years in Britain where he studied anthropology, flirted with Communism, married an English woman, and scraped a living by such shifts as acting as an extra in Alexander Korda's empire-building film *Sanders of the River*. This role he tried to forget, instead denouncing Britain's "imperialist system of slavery, tax-paying, pass-carrying and forced labour".

Kenyatta was quickly outflanked by militant young Kikuyu known as Mau Mau, meaning "greedy eaters [of elders' authority]". Essentially they were hungry for land. Bound together by secret oaths and dark rituals, they began a kind of peasants' revolt. This inflicted far more violence on their own community than on the whites, whose farms they attacked. Kenyatta condemned "bloody insurrection" but he was demonised along with the Mau Mau themselves. In 1952 he was imprisoned along with other KAU leaders.

A state of emergency was declared and a ruthless security operation was undertaken to quell what the Governor, Sir Evelyn Baring, typically regarded as a satanic reversion to savagery. It involved counter-terror often carried out by more or less licensed vigilantes. Troops, artillery, armoured cars and aircraft were deployed against the forest guerrillas. As in Malaya, massive efforts were made to isolate them from possible help, notably by resettling over a million people in gaol-villages. By 1954 70,000 Kikuyu were being held in detention camps, where many were beaten, tortured and killed. With understandable hyperbole, one historian referred to Britain's "gulag".

In 1959, when the Mau Mau was virtually defeated and its African opponents were taking up the offer of limited power-sharing with the Nairobi administration, eleven prisoners were murdered in Hola Camp. An official whitewash compounded the public outrage and Iain Macleod concluded that "we could no longer continue with the old methods of government in Africa and that meant inexorably a move towards African independence". Progress

Robert Mugabe, President of Zimbabwe, in 1982

was problematic and differences ran deep. Hard-liners among the 60,000 whites tried to insist on retaining supremacy over the six million Africans, asserting that black leaders, but for European tutelage, would still be "racing through the bush, spear in hand, dressed as the Heavenly Tailor had turned them out". But the British Treasury gave grants to buy out settlers, many of whom left. Kenyatta, who was released in 1961, proved adept at reconciliation despite his greed for power and pelf. His watchword was *Harambee* – Pull Together. In 1963 he won at the polls and became Prime Minister, leading his country to freedom – *Uhuru*.

Rhodesia's route to independence was far longer and more tortuous. This was because Rhodes had overseen an exceptionally brutal suppression of native resistance and the imposition of a white supremacy that owed much to the punitive Boer example. Moreover the settlers won virtual self-rule in 1923, which gave them control of the armed forces and the civil service, as did not happen in Kenya. Nevertheless during the 1930s Africans protested against their subjugation and after 1945 there were serious labour troubles in which the railwaymen's leader Joshua Nkomo played a prominent role. Aiming to shore up white power, Rhodesia became part of a newly formed Central African Federation (CAF) in 1953. Its other constituents were copper-rich Northern

Rhodesia (the future Zambia) and, at British insistence, poor Nyasaland. The seven million Africans, now subject to 200,000 whites, were not consulted. The CAF's eventual Prime Minister, Roy Welensky, who was described as "the Koh-i-noor of rough diamonds", said that blacks who did not cooperate would "meet the fate of the Red Indians in the USA".

Far from cooperating, African nationalists opposed the undemocratic and ill-organised CAF from the start. Their protests grew after 1956 when the price of copper plummeted, wages fell and the cost of living rose. Strikes and disturbances multiplied, especially in the two northern territories. Fearing another Mau Mau uprising, led by Kenneth Kaunda in Northern Rhodesia, by Hastings Banda in Nyasaland and perhaps by Nkomo in Southern Rhodesia, the authorities took emergency powers. They curtailed civil liberties, carried out mass arrests and imposed collective punishments. Lennox-Boyd defended the crackdown, claiming that in Nyasaland it had foiled a conspiracy to massacre whites. But an official report, produced by Lord Devlin in 1959, dismissed the "murder plot", condemned the repression and labelled Nyasaland a "police state". Macmillan was appalled, attributing Devlin's unparalleled candour to the fact that he was "Irish, lapsed Catholic and deformed".

Devlin's report, though, was the writing on the wall for the CAF. After much vacillation Macmillan agreed to a process which allowed both Kaunda and Banda to become the heads of independent states. Welensky raged that the "British Government have ratted on us" and that Macmillan's policy was "to liquidate what is left of the British Empire as quickly as possible". But Britain remained entangled in Southern Rhodesia since anti-racist opinion in the Commonwealth and the United Nations inhibited it from handing power to a white minority.

The settlers had accepted some liberalisation, such as modifying the colour bar and offering land reform, in the hope of achieving complete autonomy. But as London resisted, polarisation occurred in Salisbury. The militant Marxist Robert Mugabe eclipsed Joshua Nkomo. And in 1964 Ian Smith became leader of the governing Rhodesian Front, which was committed to white supremacy. Heckled by African students at a political meeting, he sang an Afrikaans song: "*Bobbejaan, klim die berg*" (Baboon, climb the hill).

In 1965 Smith, professing loyalty to the crown, unilaterally declared Rhodesian independence. For the next fifteen years successive Westminster governments wrestled with the thorniest of post-imperial problems. They imposed economic sanctions on Rhodesia, which were widely flouted. They tried negotiation, but Smith was both devious and intransigent. They attempted to win black support for a compromise and got "an *emphatic 'No'*".

They accepted American mediation, but though the US Secretary of State Henry Kissinger applied effective pressure on both Rhodesia and its South African backer in 1976, he still left Smith room for manoeuvre. What fatally undermined the illegal regime was an increasingly vicious and costly bush war waged by Mugabe's followers based in newly independent Mozambique. Eventually Margaret Thatcher's government obtained a cease-fire and Mugabe won the ensuing election. On 17 April 1980 he celebrated the "birthday of great Zimbabwe". Watching television pictures of the Union Jack being lowered in Salisbury and mourning the extinction of the Empire, the Iron Lady wept.

Jomo Kenyatta in the last year of his life

Chapter Fifteen

RELICS OF EMPIRE

The Empire that had grown to maturity over two centuries expired in two decades. Between 1945 and 1965 the number of people under British colonial rule shrank from 700 million to five million. Most of those who remained were in Hong Kong and others inhabited a scattering of rocks and islands all round the world, from Bermuda to South Georgia, from Pitcairn to Tristan da Cunha. Although Britannia no longer ruled the azure main, some hoped that these red dots on the map might still serve a strategic purpose and Harold Macmillan persuaded himself that "we only need our 'Gibraltars'". British influence could be sustained by a chain of cheap, defensible, sea-girt strongholds such as Ascension Island and Diego Garcia, an atoll in the Indian Ocean from which the natives were deported after 1968 to make way for a military base. They are in exile to this day and their wretched plight illustrates Britain's almost invariable disregard for the interests (not to mention the rights) of the inhabitants of its vestigial overseas territories.

The West Indies were a case in point. When their value declined with the price of sugar during the nineteenth century, they became a prey to neglect and decay. The economy, no longer sustained by slavery, stagnated. Buildings fell into ruin. Malnutrition was rife. A late-Victorian Royal Commission described the condition of British islands as "usually deplorable and sometimes

*Queen Elizabeth II and Commonwealth leaders
at the 1960 Commonwealth Conference, Windsor Castle*

desperate". Primary schooling was the worst in the Empire and well into the
twentieth century most West Indians remained illiterate. Few Britons paid
much attention to their overseas possessions despite drum-beating commercial advertisements and flag-wagging official propaganda, such as the British
Empire Exhibition (1924-5) and the British Council (1934). Most thought
that the West Indies were something to do with India and only took note of
them because the brilliant cricketer Learie Constantine hailed from Trinidad.

Whitehall barely limited the oppressive power of white oligarchies in the
Caribbean backwater, which led to frequent gusts and occasional storms of
black unrest. The worst occurred at Jamaica's Morant Bay in 1865, when
unemployed ex-slaves revolted and Governor Edward Eyre reacted with such
brutality as to provoke a bitter controversy in England. More widespread disturbances took place during the 1930s, when wages were depressed to the
level of the 1830s. Nationalist leaders emerged from this strife, many of them
socialists and trade unionists, none more flamboyant than the Jamaican Alexander Bustamante, who boasted that, if he so directed, his supporters "would
vote for a dog".

During the Second World War Churchill used the West Indies as bargaining chips, handing over island bases to the United States in return for fifty old destroyers. After 1945 Attlee's government aimed to shed costs and disengage altogether from the region. Progress was made towards widening the franchise and developing representative institutions. But most islands were deemed too weak to stand alone and protracted negotiations took place to create a union. In 1958 ten islands (Jamaica, St Kitts, Antigua, Montserrat, Dominica, St Lucia, Barbados, St Vincent, Grenada and Trinidad) merged to form the West Indies Federation. This could not survive pressure for complete independence, especially from its two strongest constituents, Jamaica and Trinidad. They became sovereign states in 1962, precipitating the dissolution of what Bustamante, Jamaica's first Prime Minister, called "the farcical Federation". Smaller islands were retained as dependencies, some prized as tax havens, others surviving as tourist resorts. Most were gradually set adrift, British imperial flotsam in what had increasingly become an American lake.

After Fidel Castro's revolution in 1959, however, Cuba became a Communist redoubt opposed to Uncle Sam's "coca-colanisation". At the height of the Cold War, this was an unbearable affront and successive occupants of the White House took measures to scotch the Red peril in Cuba and elsewhere in the Caribbean. Thus John F. Kennedy's government, which regarded the premier of British Guiana Teddi Jagan as another Castro, induced Macmillan to delay self-rule and impose a new electoral system that would deny him power. The CIA helped to undermine Jagan by fomenting strikes and riots, and in 1964 he was defeated by a right-wing coalition which took Guiana to independence. Similarly Ronald Reagan invaded Grenada in 1983 to avert what seemed like a Communist takeover. The Pentagon claimed that the operation, code-named Urgent Fury, was conducted with surgical precision even though US forces mistakenly attacked a lunatic asylum, killing thirty mental patients. American diplomacy was equally crude, Margaret Thatcher only being told at the last minute about the invasion of a Commonwealth country. She fumed privately but did not publicly condemn Reagan's action, tacitly accepting the total eclipse of British ascendancy in what he called "the great American archipelago".

In any case Mrs Thatcher owed much to Reagan for his assistance during the war over the Falkland Islands, specks in the South Atlantic which she was unable to locate on the map. British governments, which had long regarded these bleak remnants of Empire as an expensive embarrassment, made intensive efforts to discard them, preferably by arrangement with neighbouring Argentina which laid passionate claim to *Las Malvinas*. These efforts were frustrated by the islands' 1,800 inhabitants, a motley population whose chief source of income, other than their 500,000 sheep, came from the sale of stamps. Fearful of being sold up the River Plate, they were resolved to remain under the Union Jack.

Thus the principle of self-determination, which had cut at the root of the British Empire, now obliged the mother country to take responsibility for her unwanted offspring. Nevertheless Mrs Thatcher gave every indication of washing her hands of the Falklands, notably by imposing naval cuts which made their defence problematic. Thus encouraged, the fascistic military junta in Buenos Aires led by General Leopoldo Galtieri seized the islands in April 1982.

In the ensuing negotiations the Iron Lady bent, reluctantly accepting a compromise. Luckily for her, Galtieri rejected it. She then showed her mettle and her metal, which Tory nationalist Enoch Powell later assayed as "ferrous matter of the highest quality". Mrs Thatcher dispatched a "Task Force" of 28,000 men to expel the Argentinians. They put up strong resistance but on 14 June their commander in Port Stanley surrendered. The war cost Britain 255 lives and £2 billion. This was a heavy expenditure to recapture islands that Britain had tried so hard to jettison and which Denis Thatcher, when he saw them, described as "miles and miles of bugger all". The incongruity was obscured by the euphoria of victory and the crescendo of neo-colonial jingoism, summed up in the *Sun* newspaper's headline celebrating the sinking of the Argentine cruiser *General Belgrano* (with the loss of 323 sailors): GOTCHA. Margaret Thatcher herself proclaimed that the Falklands triumph had dissolved the "secret fears" of her compatriots that "Britain was no longer the nation that had built an Empire and ruled a quarter of the world".

Puffed up by hubris, Mrs Thatcher fantasised about holding on to Hong Kong after the lease of its vital surrounding New Territories ran out in 1997. Her wish to do so was understandable since Britain's last major crown colony had become an immensely rich industrial, commercial and financial centre. By the 1980s this neon-lit, skyscraper-dominated, wealth-generating machine exported more than China and four times as much as India. Critics dubbed Hong Kong, where an ossified, pith-helmeted administration fostered unbridled capitalism, as "the sweatshop of Asia". Travel brochures preferred to call it "the pearl in the dragon's mouth". China, which could have swallowed it at a gulp, preferred the taste of money to the risk of indigestion. But there was no mistaking the Communist government's determination to take back what was in effect the remaining treaty port, a symbol of China's burning humiliation at the hands of barbarous western imperialists. This became evident when Mrs

Thatcher visited Peking in 1982, where Deng Xiaoping offended her both by refusing to budge and by making generous use of the Great Hall of the People's white enamel spittoon.

After much chafing the Prime Minister bowed to the inevitable and in 1984 agreement was reached that Hong Kong would be handed over to China in 1997, to become a Special Administrative Region. This meant that it would enjoy limited autonomy and free enterprise for fifty years, thus embodying Deng's longstanding principle, "one country, two systems". The period leading up to the transfer of sovereignty was marked by corrosive mutual mistrust. This intensified in 1989, when the character of the regime to which Hong Kong would be consigned was made manifest by its massacre of hundreds (perhaps thousands) of pro-democracy demonstrators in Peking's Tiananmen Square. Relations were further embittered during the 1990s when Hong Kong's last British governor, Chris Patten, introduced new representative structures and tried to embed human rights in Hong Kong law.

These were high-minded but belated endeavours to compensate for one and a half centuries of arbitrary imperial rule. As Patten himself acknowledged, members of the Chinese Politburo suspected that he was attempting to construct a "democratic time bomb to blow their system to smithereens". They denounced him as a "dirty trickster", "tango dancer", "triple violator" and "sinner for a thousand generations".

Nevertheless there was no alternative but to ring down the curtain on the British Empire with as much aplomb as possible. The obsequies were staged on 30 June 1997. The usual parades, fanfares, pyrotechnics and flag raisings and lowerings took place. Dignitaries made orations in English and Mandarin, languages which few in Hong Kong understood. Most of its people were apprehensive, though no marketing opportunity was to be lost – hawkers sold tee-shirts announcing "The Great Chinese Takeaway" and spray cans of "colonial air" labelled "The Last Gasp of Empire".

The British were lachrymose in the monsoon rain – it was said that the heavens wept. Chris Patten certainly shed tears. Margaret Thatcher sat stony-faced. The new Prime Minister Tony Blair felt a tug of "nostalgia for the old British Empire". Prince Charles, who indiscreetly described the Chinese leaders as "appalling old waxworks", lamented the loss of the last imperial "jewel in the British Crown". As the Governor's party embarked on the royal yacht *Britannia* he was filled with "a kind of exasperated sadness". Now old and faded, this vessel was the symbol of a vanished age. And she was sailing on her final voyage before being decommissioned, to become a Scottish tourist attraction. The band of the Royal Marines played "Rule, Britannia".

The satirical magazine Private Eye mocked the Sun's jingoism with a spoof competition entitled "Kill an Argie and Win a Metro"

CONCLUSION

Euthanised by pragmatic London governments, the British Empire experienced what the historian Ronald Hyam called "a quiet and easy death". Despite the travails chronicled above, its end was peaceful compared, say, with the final convulsions of French rule in Vietnam and Algeria. In life, too, Britain's empire was gentler than that of France, as well as those of Portugal, Spain, Holland and Germany. Certainly it bore no resemblance to the "vampire empire" created by King Leopold of the Belgians in the Congo, which was responsible for the extermination of perhaps ten million people, let alone to the genocidal Nazi empire or to Japan's sadistic and kleptocratic Greater East-Asia Co-Prosperity Sphere. Even such a stern critic as George Orwell acknowledged that the British Empire was better than any other. Commenting on the handover of Hong Kong, the conservative writer Allan Massie maintained that the Empire had been an unrivalled force for good. Western Europe had lived on the legacy of Rome, he said, and "our Empire leaves at least as rich a legacy to the whole world."

It did, indeed, have much to its credit. In theory if not always in practice, it was a liberal empire. It subscribed to the ideals of freedom, free speech, good governance, representative institutions and the rule of law. It clung to Burke's belief in colonial trusteeship, cherishing its responsibility to nurture subject peoples, however slowly, towards maturity and autonomy. The Empire took its "civilising mission" seriously, working to eradicate such customs as thuggee, suttee, foot-binding, infanticide, slavery, cannibalism and human sacrifice. Preaching Christian values, it imparted ideas and skills vital to colonial emancipation. Anticipating the present globalised economy, it was an agent of modernisation, fostering commerce, spreading prosperity and providing financial stability.

British empire-builders improved communications, created industries and developed agriculture. They promoted health, education and social welfare. They encouraged sport and culture, spreading notions of fair play and helping to make English what Latin had once been, a common language. They set new standards of space and time, defining frontiers and measuring by the clock instead of the seasons. And they undertook multifarious public works, constructing on a gargantuan scale. The imperial edifice they raised is now, as Kipling forecast, "one with Nineveh and Tyre". But their influence lives on, permeating especially the eighty or so of today's 195 nation states that were once ruled or occupied by Britain.

Yet the red on the imperial balance sheet overshadowed the black. Westminster politicians might claim, as Lloyd George did in 1921, that the British Empire was unique because "Liberty is its binding principle." But this was cant designed to conceal its brutal realities. As George Orwell said, the Empire was "a despotism with theft as its final object". It was largely acquired by force, ultimately governed by coercion and subject to systematic exploitation. Opposition to British rule was invariably met by violence, sometimes by insensate cruelty as happened during the Indian Mutiny. "Lesser breeds" were victims of homicide, if not mass slaughter justified by a bastard Darwinism, as in the Antipodes. In 1883 a colonial governor reported to Gladstone that refined Queenslanders talked approvingly "not only of the wholesale butchery (for the iniquity of that may sometimes be disguised from themselves) but of the individual murder of natives". In war and peace, the British treated their colonies as a source of plunder. Between Plassey and Waterloo, for example, they extracted perhaps a billion pounds from India, a heavenly gift, according to the Earl of Chatham, which spelled the redemption of Britain.

The catalogue of imperial iniquity is yet more extensive. It includes monstrous abuses such as the slave trade and the indentured labour traffic; cases of acquisitive aggression such as the opium wars and the rape of Matabeleland; acts of wanton destruction such as the burning of the Emperor's Summer Palace at Peking and the dynamiting of the Mahdi's tomb at Omdurman; squalid fiascos such as the Jameson Raid and the Suez invasion; crimes such as the use of dum-dum bullets and poison gas; massacres such as occurred at Amritsar,

Batang Kali and Hola Camp. Torture and racial discrimination were endemic throughout the Empire. Sins of omission were equally obtrusive, notably successive failures in the duty of care for the victims of famine. Most imperial officials, who had the vices of their virtues, supported the status quo whatever its transgressions. Intensely conventional, they served their own interests and those of the authorities. Often arrogant, supercilious bullies, they seldom lived up to the pukka sahib's code, which Orwell dismissed as slimy humbug. The philosopher Bertrand Russell went so far as to call the Empire "a cesspool for British moral refuse".

To be sure, all empires govern irresponsibly since they lack the legitimacy afforded by popular consent. As Edward Gibbon wrote, "A more unjust and absurd constitution cannot be devised than that which condemns the natives of a country to perpetual servitude, under the arbitrary dominion of strangers." So it is not surprising that the British Empire betrayed the civilised values it claimed to espouse and that it destroyed or concealed large amounts of documentary evidence which would have attested to that betrayal. Nor is it any wonder that the Empire heedlessly cut at the root of indigenous cultures and drew lines on maps of India, Africa and the Middle East that still cause havoc in the world today. It is no accident that failed states and internecine strife form such a salient part of the imperial legacy.

Its consequences for Britain itself were also less than happy. The post-war arrival of "dark strangers" from colonial countries was unpopular, governments soon imposed curbs on Commonwealth immigration and the emergence of a multi-cultural society was all too often treated as a problem rather than a boon. The Commonwealth itself seemed to have little function other than to sustain British prestige by disguising the decay of British power. Enoch Powell described it as "a sticking plaster for the wound left by the amputation of empire". But phantom feelings after its loss persist. At a personal level they inspire crass sentiments on high: the Duke of Edinburgh at Amritsar contesting an Indian estimate of the death toll; Prime Minister Gordon Brown in East Africa urging his compatriots to be proud of the Empire; Foreign Secretary Boris Johnson at Yangon's Shwedagon Pagoda intoning Kipling's line, "Come you back, you English soldier." More significantly, politicians promoting chauvinistic causes such as the attack on Iraq and the campaign to leave the European Union, could tap atavistic longings for the glory days of Greater Britain. The Empire is a ghost which haunts the British psyche, subverting a sense of national identity and even purpose. Dean Acheson's aphorism, formulated in 1962, has become a cliché but it remains true to this day: "Britain has lost an Empire and has not yet found a role."

FURTHER READING

The fullest account of the subject treated here is Wm. Roger Louis (general editor) *The Oxford History of the British Empire* (Oxford, 5 volumes, 1998-9), which is accompanied by a number of companion volumes on key subjects such as science, technology, architecture, Australia's empire, the end of empire in the Pacific, and Britain's experience of empire in the twentieth century. Each of these volumes contains comprehensive bibliographies. In contrast to this academic treatment is James Morris's rich and romantic trilogy, *Heaven's Command: An Imperial Progress* (1973), *Pax Britannica: The Climax of Empire* (1975) and *Farewell the Trumpets: An Imperial Retreat* (1978). Ronald Hyam is the greatest British authority on the subject and all his books are valuable, notably the seminal essays in *Understanding the British Empire* (Cambridge, 2010). Niall Ferguson offers a robust apologia in *Empire: How Britain Made the Modern World* (2003). My own more critical narrative, of which the present work is an epitome, is *The Decline and Fall of the British Empire* (2007). A more discursive miniature is Ashley Jackson's *The British Empire: A Very Short Introduction* (Oxford, 2013). Attractive and useful volumes are Peter Marshall's *The Cambridge Illustrated History of the British Empire* (Cambridge, 1996) and Chris Bayly's *Atlas of the British Empire* (1989). Below is a brief list of further recommended reading. The place of publication is London unless otherwise stated.

Allen C. *Plain Tales from the Raj* (1976 edn.)

Anstey R. *The Atlantic Slave Trade and British Abolition, 1760-1810* (1975)

Belich J. *Replenishing the Earth: The Settler Revolution and the Rise of the Angloworld 1780-1930* (Oxford, 2008)

Cain P. J. and Hopkins, A. G. *British Imperialism* 2 vols (1993)

Calder A. *Revolutionary Empire: The Rise of the English-Speaking Empire from the Fifteenth Century to the 1780s* (1981)

Cannadine D, *Ornamentalism: How the British Saw Their Empire* (2001)

Darwin J. *Unfinished Empire: The Global Expansion of Britain* (2013)

Gallagher J. *The Decline, Revival and Fall of the British Empire* (Cambridge, 1982)

Headrick D. R. *The Tools of Empire* (New York, 1981)

Hobsbawm E. J. *Industry and Empire* (1969 edn.)

Hyam R. *Britain's Imperial Century* (1993 edn.)

Hyam R. *Empire and Sexuality: The British Experience* (Manchester, 1990)

Louis W. R. *Ends of British Imperialism* (2006)

Porter, B. *The Lion's Share: A Short History of Imperialism 1850-1983* (1984)

Robinson R. and Gallagher, J. *Africa and the Victorians* (1965)

Springhall J. *Youth, Empire and Society* (1977)

Thornton A. P. *The Imperial Idea and its Enemies* (1959)

INDEX

Note: *italics refers to images.*

10 9 8 7 6 5 4 3 2 1

ISBN 978-1-911187-85-1

First published as *All you need to know: The British Empire*
by Connell Publishing in 2018

Picture credits:
p.23 © Chronicle / Alamy
p.29 © Rischgitz / Getty Images
p.88 © Chronicle / Alamy
p.103 © Paul Schutzer/The LIFE Picture Collection/Getty Images

Design: Ben Brannan
Typesetting: Paul Woodward
Picture research: Flora Connell
Edited by Jolyon Connell